Free Me with the Truth

Krystal Fletcher

Dedication

This book is dedicated to my children. You guys motivated me to finish what I have started. You are the reasons why I couldn't give up on myself or you. I pushed myself every day to show you anything you want to do in life you can with hard work, dedication, motivation and no excuses. Put GOD first, believe in yourself and everything else will fall into place.

Acknowledgements

I would like to show my appreciation
towards the people who supported me
and helped me throughout this journey
without you this wouldn't be possible:
God, Sean Maxwell, Vicki Muhammad.
You'll have been a great part of my life
in which my dreams finally came true
and for that I will always be grateful.

Chapter 1

"Just the Beginning"

Keisha is one of the top Real Estate Brokers in Washington, DC. She owns one of the most established real estate companies called "Keisha's Luxury Real Estate" for the past five years, but actually been in this line of work over nine years.

Just when Keisha thought everything was going according to her plans at work and family life. After a long day of work she stops at the local grocery store to pick up some necessary items for dinner. She received an unknown call while in the grocery store. There was another woman on the other end of the phone.

"May I speak to Keisha?"
This is her "How may I help you"? (In Keisha's head she thought this may be

one of her clients).

Hello! Are you still there? Is this i
reference to one of the houses you may
have seen? Keisha asked.

No! "But it's about your husband". My
husband??? Why are you calling about
my husband; and how do you know
him? Keisha asked with concern.

Well not to burst your bubble but I'm
pregnant by Tim. He didn't mention it
to you. Unknown woman said.

What the hell you just say. You're
pregnant by my husband. Why would
he tell me he has a hoe pregnant?
Keisha responded in frustration. Well
Tim is the father, and I will be having
our baby in 4 months.

Hello! "Are you still there with a laugh
to follow behind." Unknown woman
said in a sarcastic way.

Bitch! I'm still here. Keisha said loudly.
As Keisha got quiet again trying to
understand what she just heard while
standing in the store. After a long

pause she hung up on the "THOT."

Keisha is now trying to figure out if this is true; things have been going "Great" in her marriage for the last seven years.

People walking up to her "Are you ok ma'am?" While she was staring into space with a basket filled with groceries in her hand. A few seconds later she snapped out of it, "Yes! I'm fine."

She debating to leave the groceries in the store, anticipating doing 95mph all the way home and fucking Tim up for what she just heard. Or she can get the groceries to feed her and Tim four children.

After leaving the store Keisha's mind is racing hundred thoughts per second. So instead of going directly home. She stopped at the local Dollar store to purchase a gift bag, pregnancy test, gift tissue paper.

Keisha is on a revenge mission as she thinks about how Tim let seventeen years go down the drain. As she thought about it the madder, she became.

Oh, I got something for that ass; Keisha said to herself, as she reaches for her phone to call her homegirl, best friend for over twenty years.

Hey! Tiffany, Are you busy?

No! What's up, it sounds like something is wrong.

You know me all too well there's something wrong, but I will tell you later, Keisha said.

I will be at your place in 10 minutes.

Ok! See you soon, Tiffany spoke curiously.

As Keisha pulled into Tiffany's driveway, she couldn't get out the car fast enough with the Dollar store bag in hand. She walked into Tiffany's house in a rage but not overly emotional because Tiffany is the kind of friend that's ready all the time to beat a bitch ass.

At this point Tiffany is three months pregnant so I didn't want to get her upset with my unbelievable news about Tim.

Are you going to tell me what's wrong? Tiffany asked.

Not at the moment I need to deal with it first, Keisha said.

You can help me out by peeing on this for me. Keisha stated.

As Tiffany had her back turned in the kitchen pouring Keisha a cup of Patron.

Pee on what Keisha, that's some nasty ass shit you asking me to do.

Tiffany responded. Bitch! I'm talking about this pregnancy test if you turn the fuck around and look.

Oh, shit bitch! Why do you have a pregnancy test? Tiffany asked with a smile on her face.

Girl it's a long story and long day. Keisha said emotionless.

I know you and Tim have been trying to have another baby recently, but it's been exceedingly difficult. Since you have been diagnosed with Lupus the kind that affects the fetus if medication is not taken.

Yeah, I know Tiffany. That's why I can't believe this low-down dirty dog of a husband I have.

Keisha, Do I need to get my Vaseline, put my Timberland boots on, and put my rings on my fingers and beat the hell out of him.

Girl, your pregnant calm down before you upset the baby. I will handle Tim.

Okay! You know I will blow his car up on 295 parkway and the police will think it's an accident. Tiffany said in her serious voice.

Bitch! I know you will, but I will handle it like I said.

Can you just go pee on the damn stick? Tiffany took the test and proceeded to the bathroom.

Keisha sits on the couch waiting patiently drinking her Patron; her phone rings: guess who it is Tim.

Hello! Keisha answered.

Hi! Baby, You still at work? Tim asks

No! Why? Keisha replied.

Can you pick up something for dinner?
Tim asked.

I already did when I left work. Keisha
said smartly.

You always know what I'm thinking.
Tim said in a loving way.

You sure about that Tim.

What do you mean by that Keisha?

You could be with someone for years
and never know them.

Ladybug, I really don't understand.

But you will very soon Keisha told Tim.

I have a gift for you Tim.

What kind of gift I know you didn't buy
me the 1961 Chevrolet Corvette that I
always wanted?

Nope! Better than that, I'll see you
when I get there.

Ok! Love you Keisha with no reply back.

Keisha yelled at Tiffany, are you done

yet?

Girl give me a second you know pregnant people move slow as they both laughed.

So, what are you going to do with the test? Tiffany's curious mind wanted to know. Well first I'll wrap it in the beautiful tissue paper that says, "You're the father". Place it in the bag and hand it to Tim when I get home.

Girl I wish I could be the fly on that wall this shit is about to blow up in his face KA-BOOM with her animated antics.

For real Tiffany this is my husband and marriage at stake.

Sorry sis! I understand but he should've thought about it before he did his dumb shit. As much as I wanted to tell Tiffany to "shut the hell up" she was absolutely right. I finished with the gift bag, picked my purse up, gave Tiffany a hug and walked to my car.

Tiffany yelled as I started to drive off.

I'm only 2.5 seconds away with my Vaseline and Tim's. Keisha yells back through her Mercedes Benz truck window: I know, love you.

Driving from Tiffany house to Keisha home is only 30 minutes away depending on traffic. Keisha had a short time to think even though it seems so long. Luckily, it's a Friday night so the kids are off of school until Monday and Tim and I had the weekend off.

Keisha called her mom to pick up the kids by 7:30pm. So, for dinner the kids will be having carryout. Keisha really didn't have the energy to prepare dinner after all of this.

When she arrived in her driveway at 7:00pm staring at her husband's truck, his most prize possession thinking about all the different ways to fuck it up. But she knew she only had 30 minutes to get the children together before her mother arrived.

Keisha turned off the car, took the keys out of the ignition, grabbed her purse and groceries. She sat there with the driver door open while she had to put her mind and emotional state in a positive one in front of the kids. She proceeded to get up, closing the car door and walking up to the front door. As she placed the keys in the lock, she took one more deep breath before seeing her children and Tim.

She opened the door, and she heard her youngest son Alim yelling mommy, mommy, which put a smile on her face. The older children were on their phones and video games as teenagers do.

Tim was in his "Mancave" watching Scarface on his 85" T.V. with surround sound for better effects. Keisha placed her purse, keys, and groceries on the dining room table.

I told all the kids to pack their clothes because they're spending the weekend with their grandmother. Speaking of

the Devil Keisha received a text
message from her mom stating: I will
be there in 15 minutes.

Ok! See you soon. Keisha replied.

Keisha told the children that your
father and I need to spend time alone
without children. Also, I was going to
fix y'all dinner, but I got carryout
instead.

As the children were packing their
things. Tim appears from the basement
with his arms extended as if he wanted
to give me a hug, like I didn't know
what his good for nothing ass has been
up to. As I stare at him with disgust,
anger, rage, resentment: wondering
WHY, WHEN, WHERE, and WHO. I
gave him the church hug I could at
least manage until the kids left.

Babe, did you put the groceries away if
not I will, Tim asked.

No! I didn't have a chance too. Getting
the kids packed so they can spend time
with my mother. Keisha replied.

Ok! Great, now we can have some adult time with no interruptions. Tim said happily. Just when Keisha was about to respond her mom beeped the horn. "Saved by the bell" she whispered with anger.

Keisha yelled for the kids to come downstairs because it was time to go and the real show was about to happen.

Tim and I always made sure we told our kids we loved them especially when they were leaving for the weekend, but this weekend had a different purpose for Tim and I.

She grabbed her keys off the table making sure the children grabbed their food and walked to the car as she greeted her mom. Thanks mom I really appreciate you taking them at a truly short notice. Victoria (Keisha's mom) anything for you and my grandchildren love you and see you Sunday.

Keisha went to her car to get the

wonderful gift she brought Tim.

Did you blow him up yet? I will be your alibi. Tiffany text.

Bitch no not yet kids just left and you are crazy. Keisha text back. Well let me know if you need me. I will Tiffany.

Keisha mom Victoria pulls out the driveway there wasn't anything or anyone to hold her back. She opens the front door to enter her home. Baby let's run around the house naked and get into some shit, because we haven't had any alone time without the kids and our crazy work schedules. Tim said sexually.

Is there anything you need to tell me Tim?

As she presented Tim's gift.

Keisha, what are you talking about?

Open your gift as he pulled out the test he was filled with excitement.

What does this mean we're pregnant? Tim asked, no but your side chick is, Keisha responded.

So, you're just going to play with my intelligence like this; you piece of shit, low down motherfucker.

Baby, what are you talking about? Cause I really don't know.

So, you don't remember your dick falling in some bitch pussy and getting the THOT pregnant; you bitch Keisha shouted. As Keisha rage and anger took over. She picked up the closest thing to her which was the dining room table chair and threw it at him.

She was yelling I gave you all of me; mind, body, soul, 17 years, 4 kids, gave you this bomb ass pussy when you wanted. Gave you everything you needed. Glass cups, kids' toys, laptop, etc..... Was getting thrown with a strong arm as if we were playing baseball across Tim's head.

Tim shouting STOP! STOP! What the fuck are you doing? I didn't get that bitch pregnant but Yes! I did step out on you with her. Yes! I did sleep with her unprotected, but I always pulled out.

She blackout punched Tim in his mouth. He was trying to escape, there wasn't nowhere to hide. She was chasing him around with a baseball bat that she got from behind the couch, while swinging aiming at his body.

You want to be out there in the streets. I will make sure when you go this time your ass will be broken down into pieces like humpty dumpty bitch. Swinging the bat at Tim started to weigh on her arms which gave Tim time to plead his case from the "Mancave" as Keisha figured out what else she can get her hands on.

Keisha I'm sorry she didn't mean nothing. I want you, my family, we been together for 17 years. I fucked up. I'm not ready to give up.

Keisha played it cool as if she forgave him that quickly. I hear you baby no one is coming between you and I. She

enters the "Mancave" where Tim
stands with a confusing and fake ass
sorry look on his face. Tim never saw
Keisha act in such a manner, but Tim
ass was overdue. She tells Tim baby it
would all be over, and we can move
forward if you just be honest.
How long were you sleeping with her?
Keisha asked.
About 7 months. Tim answered with
his hands covering his face.
Do you love her? Keisha demanded an
answer.
No! I have feelings for her. Tim replied.
Do you want to be with her? Keisha
asked.
Hell no!!! Tim answered looking at
Keisha.
Keisha whispers in his ear "Thank you"
for being honest, Round 2
motherfucker. She kneed him in the
dick he went down like Frazier. His face
met this 2 piece with an uppercut. All I
could hear was "Stomp his ass out" in

Tiffany's voice.

Keisha finally got tired of fighting, she told him to get the fuck out. Tim begging, pleading, telling her all of the sweet nothing.

I don't give a fuck "Get the hell out my house" Keisha said.

She left the "Mancave" walking towards what was ours now just her bedroom. She sat on the bed, tears falling, asking herself how she missed the signs. As she turned her head towards the closet on the left side of the bed Tim Hennessy was sitting on the nightstand. She reached for the Hennessy and cracked it open and started to drink it. Now she sees why her husband drinks Hennessy, it gets you right. Keisha gets up off the bed just when she was about to start blaming herself for the infidelity her husband caused.

She flung the closet doors open grabbing all Tim's clothes, shoes, hats, belts and anything that belonged to him went into the bonfire in our backyard as much as this wouldn't take the pain away forever. It did feel good to pour gasoline on his shit and watch it burn. Tim must've waited for me to leave the room so he can gather some of his things to leave until he realizes his shit was gone, a smell in the air of BBQ in the backyard.

As Keisha looks over Tim's clothes being destroyed. She hears him yell "Keisha is that my shit you burning"? Indeed, it is bitch made motherfucker, ungrateful, less than a man, dirt on the bottom of my shoe's bastard. What you thought it was a BBQ with food, Nope! it's all your prized possession. "NOW GET THE HELL OUT" before I fuck your truck up to do you understand.

I'm really sorry I didn't mean to hurt you.

Keisha started to count 10, 9, 8, 7, 6, 5, 4 by the time she got to 3 you heard him speeding up the street. Black tires marks on the driveway pavement a cloud of smoke from the burning tire marks following behind him.

She went back into the house and looked at all the damage. She was still mad drinking Tim's Hennessy. The only thing besides her family that calms her down is the love of music. As she dances in the living room while crying and thinking her marriage is over. Falling on the couch drinking her sorrows away she eventually fell asleep. Saturday morning was kind of a better start beside the hangover Keisha is enduring. She knew cleaning the house would take her mind off of what took place last night.

Music is still playing and one of her favorite songs is on. She could relate to every word she was singing because this was her and Tim at the beginning of their relationship. She said to herself he's no longer physically abusing me, but emotionally, mentally he is just when I thought he changed.

She began cleaning and placing things back in the correct order before her children come home tomorrow.

Just when she thought this would be the day of reflecting, Tim calls. She allows the phone to ring debating do she really want to hear him now that she's calm down. After the 10th call and 30th text message Keisha finally answered the phone and didn't speak a word.

My ladybug I know you there and I understand you don't want to talk or see me. But I'm really sorry I broke your heart into pieces with my actions of a boy not a man. I will do anything in my will power to fight for my marriage because that's what I want. Keisha tried to hold back the tears. Was I not enough for you to where you had to seek attention elsewhere?

Do you realize you had a Strong Black

Intelligent Woman? 5'10, 175 lbs., Dark Chocolate skin, body looking banging after 4 kids, Gorgeous Dark Brown eyes, shoulder length hair. Successful businesswoman took care of the home, you and the children gave you everything. You just threw it all away for 7 months and a baby to a bitch you barely even knew. To piggyback off of what you said, Yes! You are very sorry you would never find another like me. Without Tim responding Keisha hung up.

Chapter 2

"Self-Reflection"

Keisha went into the kitchen to cook some breakfast scramble eggs with spinach, wheat toast, turkey bacon and she couldn't forget the mimosa.

After a fulfilling breakfast Keisha walked upstairs, opened the door to the bathroom, looked in the mirror and asked herself "Why me". She began to torture herself with all her thoughts on how she could have stop Tim's infidelity in which is causing her so much afflictions.

She started to undress as she leaned over to the shower to turn on the hot and cold water to try and ease her mind off of things, and to really begin her day with a long jog in Buddy

Attick Park.

Keisha stepped in the warm water hitting her chocolate insane body tears filled in her dark brown eyes screaming to the top of her lungs knowing no one could hear her. After about a minute or two she started to relax as she picked up the soap and washcloth that ever so gently caresses her body in which Tim hasn't done in months; now she understands why.

She turns the water off, snatches her towel with frustration and wraps it around her beautiful shapely body. Keisha steps out of the shower brushing her teeth in the sink.

She enters her bedroom closet laying out her jogging gear, putting her smell goods on her body.

Her phone began to ring and continuously text messages began to come in. Keisha said out loud this bet not be Tim blowing my phone up. He made his bed now he's going to lay in it.

She continued to put her clothes on to get this good and well needed jog in nothing or no one was going to interrupt that.

Keisha pulled her hair into a slick ponytail, grabbing her keys, phone, credit cards as she walked downstairs. She arrived at Buddy Attick Park within 45 minutes leaving her home. EarPods in her ears light walking to start before the long jog, while listening to her playlist. The radiant sun kisses her skin giving a beautiful glow after 5 laps around this enormous park with a gorgeous view of the lake.

She headed back to her truck where she left her phone. Only to be greeted with 35 miss calls and 60 text messages. Keisha finally opened her messages 15 from Tiffany asking what happened and did I go through with blowing his shit up. The rest is from him. Keisha didn't want to speak his name, he no longer deserved that.

She texted, Tiffany Yes! I went through with it, but this is a sensitive topic. How will I tell our children their father no longer lives with us?

You shouldn't, he should. He created this turmoil within the household. Tiffany replied.

Your right but I don't want to see him at all. I guess he can tell them on Monday when he picks them up for school. Keisha said.

Exactly! I love you sis. Tiff text. I know with a heart emoji. Keisha sent back. On a quiet drive back home, she realized she needed girl time so she texted back; "Can you meet me at my house for lunch in an hour?"

Hell yeah! I was waiting for you to ask me. Tiffany responded.

Keisha finally made it home rushing upstairs to take a quick shower before Tiff arrived. She hears a knock on the door as she takes her time to open the

door. She already knew it was Tiffany.
Hey girl, how have you been? Tiffany
asked.

I can't believe he would jeopardize our
family like this. Trying to keep myself
busy enough to where I don't think
about it. I guess when the kids come
home tomorrow, we will take a mini
trip to Six flags. Then when Monday
comes, I will bury my head into my
work.

Negotiating agreements for my clients
to either sell or buy different houses or
land. Which is at some point difficult
depending on the client.

You really want to hear about what
happened huh?

Yes! I do. Where is Tim? You would
think he would be here begging and
kissing your ass to get his family back,
Tiff said. I really don't care about what
Tim is or not doing, at this point.

Well long story short Tim denied it at
first, I gave him the gift bag which he

thought I was pregnant (but I kindly let him know I knew about his side chick being pregnant). Then he finally admitted that he had been having an affair for seven months and started having feelings for her.

I just lost it and proceeded to play baseball with his head. Unfortunately, I couldn't play grit ball. So, I used the next best thing, a baseball bat.

I know his ass was black and blue with a splash of purple as Keisha and Tiffany laughed. Girl, then had a bonfire in the backyard with his clothes. Bitch! You had a waiting to exhale moment.

Tiffany said damn near choking on her water.

Yes! Indeed, I did, and it felt great, but the cleanup was a pain in the ass. Girl he sped so fast out the driveway all you saw was smoke. But real talk I love my husband. I married him not so it can end in divorce. I also understand why women can't stay away.

When you see a successful black man 6'1, 215 lbs., caramel complexion, pretty green grayish eyes, body chiseled with an 8 pack, curly hair and definitely packing 10 inches in his pants. Then on top of that he owns his landscaping business that's worth millions.

But is it too much to ask of him to stay faithful to the woman he devoted his heart to before God.

As Keisha was spilling her heart out to Tiffany, she noticed that she had this puzzled look on her face. Maybe Tiff is having a moment in her marriage to KJ, while I'm throwing all my marital problems on her.

Tiff are you okay it seems that something is wrong; Am I talking too much because this isn't you to be so quiet. No! KJ and I is fine down to my law firm. Everything is going well. I just had a quick thought about something I remember, that's all.

Well glad you and KJ are not in the same boat as Tim and I.

Girl it's time to eat this smoked salmon, mash potatoes w/ gravy and grill asparagus. What would you like to drink Tiff? Just water is fine.

I still had my suspicions about Tiffany; she never kept anything from me. I really wanted to know what she remembers but I didn't want to push her to tell me, it seems to bother her. To change some of the energy in the room I lit some sage and began to walk throughout the house while playing my playlist on Alexa yes it started off with one of my favorite songs.

Tiffany waited for the song to go off and said "Keisha you need to be listening to "Papers" by Usher. That damn Tiff just when I thought her ass was on mute a glimpse of her was showing up again.

Tiffany's phone rang. I'm assuming it was KJ as abruptly she had to leave.

Beside it was around 9:00pm so I didn't mind her leaving. I now needed my alone time.

Chapter 3

"Family Outing"

Keisha took one sip of her pink Moscato, cleaned the dishes and headed to the bathroom to brush her teeth. As she slipped in some comfy pajamas and took her ass to sleep. Keisha was awakened by her cell phone as she reached to answer without paying attention to who was calling.

Hello! Keisha answered.

Good Morning Baby! Tim said.

Keisha quickly realizes this is not her mom calling.

Hello! Good Morning Baby, Tim said.

As much as Keisha wanted to hear her husband's voice she couldn't bare too.

Bye Tim.

The phone rang again Keisha just knew

Tim was calling back. She answered: What the fuck do you want Tim? Victoria (Keisha's mom) responded I'm not Tim and the kids will be there by 2:00pm. Sorry mom I didn't mean it. I thought you were Tim, Keisha said. I kinda figured that, the way you answered the phone, Victoria said. I just knew I couldn't go back to sleep so I walked downstairs to make sure everything was in order before the children came home and didn't want them to suspect anything happened between their father and I. I didn't want Tim and I problems to become our children's problem. For some reason, the clock seems so loud Keisha pacing the floor hoping that the kids didn't notice Tim is not there. How would I explain it to them or should I. 2 o'clock rolled around my mom is always on time as Keisha opens the front door she was pulling up. I was so excited to see my kids and mom which was a breath of fresh air.

Did y'all have fun with grandma?
Keisha asked.

Yes! We did but we were glad to be
home. All the kids replied.

Thanks, mom, for everything, Keisha
said with gratitude.

Anytime baby that's what I'm here for
even a listening ear, Victoria replied. At
the same time, we both said love you as
we went our separate ways.

Hey children, can you come to the
living room? I have a great idea. Yes!
Ma what is your great idea? Keisha's
daughter Johnaya asked. Well, I was
thinking we would have some fun at
Six Flags today if you wanted to go.
3 out of 4 children replied "let's go"
but my oldest Khalif said he's not
interested which I could understand he
is 16.

Okay! We will be leaving in 10 minutes
please make sure you have everything
you need.

As 10 minutes pass Keisha has her keys, purse, phone and Six Flags tickets she purchases online, while standing in the open doorway of the front door.

Let's go kids (Keisha shouted).

Love you Khalif we will be back soon. Please answer your phone when I call. Don't have your headphones up to loud where you can't hear. We all loaded into my truck driving 45 minutes to Six Flags. My youngest son Alim was so excited to see Bugs Bunny, Tweety Bird, etc..... To be honest this was keeping my mind off the fact Tim is having a baby with another woman. Three hours passed, and we all were so exhausted ready to go home, and crash into our beds but not before eating dinner, showering and brushing our teeth.

We all need to be well-rested because Lord knows tomorrow is going to be a long day. Tim is coming in the morning to pick up the kids for school.

Chapter 4

"Better to be on Time"

Keisha Text Tim:

Please make sure you on time tomorrow

Be here by 8:00am
Kids can't be late for school.
School starts at 9:15am

Tim Text Keisha Back:

Yeah, I will be there by 8
Can we talk after I drop the kids at school

Keisha replied:

Nope! I think you did enough talking.
Just be here by 8.
6:30am–Keisha's alarm clock goes off.
7:00am– Keisha took her morning shower.
7:15am– Keisha enters her kids room

shouting rise and shine porcupine.

7:20am – Cooking breakfast

7:30am – Kids getting dress for school.

7:45am – Time for everyone to eat.

As time gets closer Keisha starts to get expressive. Mom! Where is dad? Normally he is at the table. Keisha's son Khalif asked. Keisha knew someone was going to ask. As she searches for the words to speak. She answered he will be here by 8 to take you to school. Three minutes later we all turned our heads towards the door where Tim was walking in. Well, I'm going upstairs to get dressed for work. Kids leave your plates on the table and go brush your teeth. It's time to go. Make sure you have everything you need for school. Good Morning Keisha. (Tim Spoke) That's the problem: my morning was good before I saw you (Keisha mumble under her breath).

From upstairs Keisha hears her son Elliott ask: Dad! Where are you coming from, and why wasn't you home yesterday?

That's between your mother and I son. Let's go!! Traffic is crazy in the morning especially on Kenilworth Ave. -Door shut.

Keisha took a deep breath as a sigh of relief that Tim didn't get into details. She rushed to the kitchen to clean the dishes from breakfast as quickly as she could. I can't be late for work. She grabbed everything off the table zoomed out the door. This will be a long drive to work especially because people didn't know how to drive.

Chapter 5

"Workplace"

She arrived 20 minutes before her office was to open. Luckily, her receptionist Angel and Assistant Tanya were already there getting things together. They knew I needed coffee. All I could smell was the aroma of Harry and David milk chocolate caramel coffee.

As Keisha placed her things in the office. She came out to pour a cup of coffee and to talk to the ladies.

Hey Ladies, how was your weekend?

I caught up on some sleep. Tanya spoke.

For me I was at the club Friday and Saturday and you know on Sunday I was in church praising the Lord, Angel said.

At the same time Tanya and I said child you are a mess, but we couldn't expect more out of Angel she was only 22 living her best life.

In Keisha quiet thoughts she wanted to be free and careless just like Angel like she was before she met Tim. Tanya and Angel said you didn't answer Ms. Keisha. "How was your weekend?

"Restless– Keisha replied as she walked into her office drinking her coffee. Angel and Tanya knew when Keisha walked into her office it was time to get to work.

Mr. & Mrs. Johnson was Keisha's client in matters of fact her favorite clients. They were very upbeat, funny, laughing at each other corny jokes. Keisha placed their property up for sale located on Macarthur Blvd N.W. Washington, DC. Five bedrooms, four bathrooms, two half bathrooms, 4,000 sqft, and priced at $2,380,000. Keisha commission would be over $50,000 so she was

excited for someone to make an offer.
Just as Keisha was finishing up her
phone calls with her clients and
realtors.

Angel buzzes Keisha on the intercom.
Your husband Tim is in the waiting
area.

Tell him I'm not here. (Keisha said).

He can hear you, Mrs. Keisha.

Ok! Just tell him to meet me outside.

No problem (Angel responded).

Mr. Jones, Mrs. Keisha said she will
meet you outside.

Ok! As Mr. Jones (Tim) started to walk
out the office.

Keisha had to gather her thoughts and
emotions because she was at work. It
didn't look professional having her
husband in her office arguing with him.
She met Tim outside.

Tim flooded her with flowers, gifts,
chocolate, money in a card thinking
that would make shit better. Why are
you not at work and why are you here?

Keisha asked. I have employees for that, besides, I want my wife back. Fuck you and what you want I'm done.

Tim begging, grabbing Keisha hands I fucked up how can I make things right. You can't and goodbye our only communication is our children don't come back to my place of business. So, you're just going to give up on 17 years. Tim had the nerve to ask Keisha. Nope! But you did when you fucked another bitch and got her pregnant. So, look in the mirror and ask your damn self that same question. Get in your car and leave. Bye I'm going back to work.

As Keisha goes back to work Tanya and Angel asks; You okay boss lady? Yes! I am and go back to work. We have tons of work to do and my personal business is not 1, Keisha said.

Chapter 6

"Cookout Secrets and

Betrayals"

Several months had gone by since Tim and Keisha really spoken. Tim was continuing sending flowers, chocolate and anything he could think of to her office and their home they once shared. Tim should be focusing on the baby he just had. It's been over 4 months. Tiffany called Keisha "What are you doing this weekend especially on Saturday?

Nothing much the kids going over to their friend's house Saturday afternoon. Why?

KJ cooked on the grill and we invited some people over. You know I'm there

KJ can cook his ass off.

What time Tiffany?

3 pm

Do I need to bring anything? Keisha asked.

Nope! We have everything covered.

Ok! See you soon.

Keisha work week has been very hectic and seems awfully long.

Saturday morning came. Keisha is thrilled to finally be around adult company. But to only think if Tim was invited as well, since KJ and Tim are incredibly good friends.

She starts to pour a cup of red wine just to ease the thought while laying her outfit out on the bed. There's no way Tiffany invited Tim. Everyone eventually was dressed, packed and ready to go. Keisha drove each child to their friend's house.

Of course, her son Elliott wanted to hear young people's music, for some reason the music that was on in his head is for old folks. Elliott let me know he talked to his father. He asked ``How were you doing?''. Oh! He did huh, Keisha replied.

After all the kids were dropped off it was time for Keisha to be entertained, never know who I will meet. Tiffany sometimes has different characters coming to her gathering so you never know what you're going to get.

She finally pulled up but there wasn't anywhere to park. So, she had to drive around a couple of times until this blue Honda freed the parking space she pulled into.

Luckily, the walk wasn't too far Keisha made sure to dress extremely comfortable but sexy. Black sheer low cut bodysuit w/ Dark Blue high waist jeans with her 6-inch heels. Just in case her feet started to hurt in her purse were them old faithful sandals. She knocked on Tiffany's door with no answer, but the door was unlocked.

Keisha walked in and no one was in sight, so she went through the kitchen to get to the backyard yelling Tiffany name. She finally answer I'm by the grill Keisha.

Tiff and KJ were marinating the chicken before placing it on the grill. There was a crowd of people there laughing, dancing, playing spades just enjoying themselves.

Keisha let's plan a trip somewhere like Paris; Tiff said with excitement. Before she could answer some loud ass girl, walked in talking to someone but we couldn't see the person.

Where are the drinks at Tiffany? The young lady asked.

On the table by Mika (Tiffany answered).

Anyway Tiffany, that would be a great girl's trip lord knows I need it. Just let me know when. Girl I got you. Tiff told Keisha.

Keisha went to help Tiffany bring the

food out to KJ. Just when Keisha slid
the patio door to walk out. She sees
Tim with the loud ass girl that came in.
Really for real this is what we doing.
What's wrong Keisha?
You had the nerve to invite Tim and
he's here with some random.
No! The fuck I didn't and KJ didn't
either Tiffany said.
So how he knows about the BBQ then
if you didn't tell him.
Tim never notice that Keisha was
there, she approach him "Is this what
the fuck you doing"? Tim knew he was
caught again as if he was caught off
guard.
KJ whispers to Tiffany shit is about to
go down.
Baby, "Who is this"? Random asked
Tim.
I'm his fucking wife "Who are you?".
The woman that called your phone
several months ago.
Tim, this the side chick that was

pregnant.

Tim put his hands on his head full of guilt. Yes! Keisha.

You are still up to your good for nothing ways, begging me to let you back home, constantly sending gifts telling me you wanted your family and marriage back. You are a poor excuse for a man. I would knock the shit out of you, but you are not worth my time; the lord saved your life.

So, Brittany when I saw Tim over your house cutting your lawn; you was sleeping with him? Tiffany asked.

Yup! Every time he came over.

KJ brings Tim the whole bottle of Cîroc you're going to need this man. You really fucked up this time. KJ told Tim.

Brittany shut the hell up; Tim angrily said.

You put the capital "W" in whore Brittany; you forever sleeping with someone man.

Tiffany, do you really want to go there

because the bones in your closet; if I were you, I would keep my mouth closed.

What bones in your closet Tiffany?

What is Brittany talking about? KJ asks Tiffany.

Keisha is so pissed she looks at Tim. I'm filing for a divorce. You just like a dog chasing his tail between his legs. You want to lay with a walking STD be my guess. Divorce papers will be hand delivered by Friday morning.

I have no clue what the home wrecker is talking about KJ.

Really Tiffany so you're not going to tell him that KJ jr. isn't his; and you've been sleeping with Tim for the past 4 years behind Keisha back. Last bomb to drop KJ jr is Tim's son too, and maybe the one she is pregnant with now. But yet I'm the whore. Brittany said.

Rewind back up so KJ jr and the baby you are pregnant with now is not mine. That's what misery people do cause problems.

Answer the fucking question Tiffany, KJ yelled.

Yes! Answer the fucking question Tim, Keisha scream.

All of it is true KJ didn't want to hurt you but I needed an outlet. You never listen to me. It goes in one ear and out the other.

So, you open your legs like 7-11 or better yet Wendy's drive thru. I never cheated on you, never had the desire too. I'm a real man that doesn't cheat; you know how many times I could've, but I didn't want you to feel the same pain I'm feeling right now. But 1 thing for certain and 2 thing for sure you getting the "HELL OUT MY HOUSE". You, Tim and Brittany can figure that shit out. I'm done with your trifling ass, but KJ jr is staying here.

Keisha heard enough so Tiff that's why you were acting funny saying you remember something. Every time I looked at KJ jr he looked similar to my children, but I didn't give it any thought. KJ is 6'0 feet and 200 lbs., cinnamon complexion, hazel eyes, long locs and very handsome; I assumed that where KJ jr got his looks.

You were my shoulder to cry on the person I go to when Tim and I are having issues. After tonight lose my number, don't call, text, or drive to my house or office. I'm through with you, Brittany and Tim y'all can have each other.

Keisha, I was scared to tell you our friendship means the world to me; Tiffany said crying.

Yeah! Whatever slut: Keisha said in disbelief.

KJ stared at Tim filled with rage. We are supposed to be brothers and you slept with my wife for real.

I did; if I could take it back I would but those kids are not mine and we need a DNA test asap, Tim said pissed. What are you trying to do KJ it's not my fault your wife is a hoe? Tim said.

KJ punched Tim in the nose. Tim swung back hitting KJ. They fell on the table rolling on to the ground. Tim picks up KJ throwing him against the fence. KJ eventually gains balance and tackles Tim.

As the fight going on Keisha walks out to find Tim truck, she pulled out her knife slashing all 4 tires. She walked back into the yard finding Tiffany's water hose turning it on, spraying water on Tiffany and Brittany y'all hoes look thirsty "DRINK UP."

Chapter 7

"How to Break the News"

Next day Keisha is drained to full capacity, stressed out, going through a deep depression; trying to figure out how to get out of this dark place. The life she once knew is demolished, not getting past this, therapy couldn't help them.

All she wanted was a life that was satisfying to her; with God first, faithful husband, children, successful career, a roof over top their head, was enough for her.

Watching TV waiting for the kids to come home, only to think my godson is really my children's brother. How could either one of them betray me in such a way she was my best friend over 20 years; been there through her ups and downs never turned my back on her or better yet slept with KJ.

For Tim I guess it's true when they say "Once a cheater always a cheater" he proves that to be true. I don't understand how he doesn't see the seriousness in his action, but he will see how done I am Friday.

Tim has crossed the lines for the last time. Keisha is changing all locks to her house on Monday once she meets with her lawyer. Something needs to change and if Tim is not willing to do so Keisha is taking matters into her own hands. This is not the way I want our sons to think they're supposed to treat women and especially their wife; and my daughter doesn't need to think she needs to take this from a man, especially her husband. Not saying Tim is a bad father but he is a terrible husband.

Keisha devoted seventeen years of her life to Tim now she gotta break the news to their children; that we are getting a divorce. Wondering how that will affect the children and what steps to assure them we are still their parents and love them dearly and want the absolute best for them.

The kids are finally home going through the kitchen to find something to eat.

My boys asked in sequence:

Mom can dad come over to play basketball and video games with us?

Why? Y'all can go where your dad lives.

Just when she thought today was going to be filled with laughter and no drama.

Do you know where dad lives because we don't?

No! Does it need to be today? Keisha asked.

Yes! Mom it's been a while since dad has been home, Elliott said.

Just when she wanted to say, "HELL NO", what really came out I understand. He can come over for a couple of hours, but your father is not staying over.

Okay I will call him now. Keisha's sons replied.

Keisha continued to watch TV just when "Martin" went off; her next show came on "The Wayans Brothers" another funny show with realistic realities of life. She is crying laughing at "Marlon and Pops" when Tim walks in without knocking as if he still lives here; it's time to change the locks on Monday.

While the kids didn't have a clue, their father was here; Keisha had to run the rules down to Tim.

Rule 1: You don't live here anymore.

Rule 2: Hand over your keys

Rule 3: Only communicate we having is only for the kids.

Rule 4: No staying over.

Rule 5: Stop sending gifts.

Rule 6: Don't show up without calling.

Rule 7: Don't bring any of your hoes or

outside kids to my home.

If you can abide by my rules, we will be fine. Keisha told Tim.

Keisha for real rules, come on now this is technically still my house too. But I understand I fucked up. Your wishes have been granted. Tim walks away to find the kids as he says to Keisha, I still love you. No! You love yourself like always; go find your kids and leave me the hell alone.

She hears Tim and the kids laughing while the basketball bouncing heading to the indoor basketball court inside the house. She loves the bond he has with them; I will never come between something so precious and priceless. Two hours into Tim being there someone knocks on the door. Keisha saying to herself he broke the damn rules already typical of Tim; only to open the door there stands the delivery driver. Tim orders pizza for dinner. Keisha walks to the other side of the house to inform the kids the pizza is here. Ladybug can we have 5 more minutes we're in the middle of the basketball game, then the kids and I will come to eat dinner if you don't mind. Yeah, whatever Tim only 5 minutes then it's bedtime and your time to leave as well after dinner. Tim looked at Keisha with a smile as she rolled her eyes and walked away.

First time in a long time we actually sat down at the table as a family, despite the children having no clue about the divorce, but I must admit I kinda miss it too.

Dad! Where are you staying it seems like you never home anymore? Johnaya asks.

Well! Baby girl I'm renting myself an apartment I live in Laurel now, you and your brothers can come over anytime, I will always make time for y'all no question asked.

Since we are on the topic "Dad, what

happened the reason why you don't live here anymore"? Khalif and Alim asked.

I really don't think your mother and I want to get into the details, but I will say this I messed up as a man, now am paying for it.

In life you do stupid things, and it comes with consequences. Sorry is not always enough when you hurt the one you deeply love.

Well! Kids it's time for bed, put your plates in the sink and go brush your teeth, love you. Tim time for you to go, Keisha said.

Keisha starts to clean up after dinner; she catches Tim staring at her while gathering his things to leave. Tim really looks good especially after playing ball with the kids. His body looks really tasty right now; Damn! I want to have sex with my husband, but I just can't allow myself to do so.

She didn't want to acknowledge Tim, so, she continued to wash dishes. He walked over to her and said you are still my everything no matter if we are together or not. I truly let a great woman go due to my actions.

She hasn't spoken any words, she walked over to the front door and opened it; Tim finally got the picture walking to the door as well. He stood in the doorway as Keisha shut the door and gave her a kiss on the forehead, Goodnight Ladybug.

Chapter 8

"Closing Deals"

Several weeks later Keisha finally had an offer for Mr. & Mrs. Johnson Home $2,100,000. The offer was way under the listed price, but it was still an offer. Mr. & Mrs. Johnson was kinda disappointed, but they needed an offer soon because they were buying a vacation home in Mexico.

Would you like to close on this offer, we have a lot of potential buyers, but this is the first all cash and 10 days to close offer we had. Keisha told the Johnson's. Well, you know what an offer is better than no offer we accept. Baby we are about to be on the white sand, crystal blue water, drinking mimosa with our feet kicked up. How that sounds Mrs. Johnson perfectly fine, she replied.

Okay! Great and congratulations to you both. I will have the papers typed up in the next 2 business days. Keisha said with excitement.

Right after finishing this great call with the Johnson's. Keisha receives a text from Tiffany. Hey Keisha, I really want to explain myself. Can you answer my text please, I want my bestie back? What is there to explain? She slept with my husband and had a baby and a possible by Tim, and she fucked over a 20 years of sisterhood. Keisha said to herself while looking at the phone, she never responded back to Tiffany.

Eight months later Tim and I officially divorce after he refused to sign for at least 2 months. Starting my new journey to happiness with my children.

Chapter 9

Vegas "Sin City"

Girl's Trip

After a long battle with Tim, Keisha plans a trip to Vegas with Tanya and Angel to let her hair down for once. We finally arrived at Caesar Palace. This hotel is so beautiful it reminds you of a mini mall. We check in to our rooms, freshen up and hit the strip to see what it has to offer.

We made sure we all dress comfortable because that dry heat is no joke literally. Taking pictures of the beautiful structures. Tanya wanted to see some male strippers Angel and I was all in especially me, so we looked up some male revue spots, we came across a lot but the one with different chocolate (men) stuck out. Can't wait to be entertained Keisha said we gotta put on our freakum dress.

Angel heard a lot about this place called Sugar factory, but we never been we needed to see what the hype is about. The drinks are to die for they give you so much and are highly creative with it. We will definitely be going back before we go home. Grabbed something to eat which was worth every bit of the price. Heading back to the hotel switching into our swimwear. Tanya, "Do you see Keisha throwing back those drinks"? Angel asked.

Yes! Girl she had 6 shots under 3 minutes, hell we took the first 2 shots with her. Tanya said. This is really going to be a fun weekend Keisha said loudly. Keisha, Are you okay? You've been drinking since we got on the plane.

Yes! Angel I'm fine. Besides my divorce

is final now, this weekend is about me living life and letting go, so drink up because I'm going to get us some more drinks. I will be right back.

Tanya, did you know she was going through a divorce?

No! I'm just finding out too, well that explains a lot when Tim came to the office, she wanted to meet him outside. Tanya replied. Well, you know when someone freshly breaks up you want to turn up, so Keisha is about to have us doing all kinds of shit, so bitch get prepared. Angel told Tanya.

Look, Keisha at the bar flirting with the bartender, should we go get her, Tanya said.

No! Indeed, let her live her best life; hopefully, we get free drinks. Angel replied.

Ladies, I'm back. The handsome bartender will bring us Patron and Hennessy shots, nachos, chicken wings. We gotta get right for tonight entertainment for the male strippers, hell let's go see females' strippers if y'all don't mind.

This is all about you so we all in. Tanya and Angel responded in excitement.

Keisha, "Why didn't you tell us about your divorce"? Tanya asked. Ladies because it wasn't easy. I was with Tim for seventeen years and have four children with him. Now I don't have my forever love, besides that's my personal business that doesn't need to be broadcast.

Well, she told you nosy, Angel said laughing.

Ladies look at fine piece of chocolate right there bringing us our drinks. I meant to ask you, your name handsome. Keisha asked in a flirting manner.

My name is Brandon.

Brandon, ladies always hitting on you, you're very sexy and easy on the eyes, and you gotta be packing downstairs as

Keisha staring him up and down.

Yeah, every now and again someone tries to hit on me, and yes, I never had any complaints on my package, and I use it very well, Brandon said with that gorgeous smile.

Well Damn! The ladies said at the same time.

I might want to see later on Brandon unless you all talk. Here's my number, my actions will show you better than I can tell you beautiful, he said with confidence. Talk to you soon as Keisha bites her bottom lip. Thanks for the drinks Brandon! You're welcome Love.

Keisha, What the hell was that? Angel asked.

The party is just getting started. Let's finish our shots and food and head to our rooms for later on. Keisha said. Don't forget your freakum outfits ladies.

Yes! Ladies, we look stunning and beautiful as ever. Tanya wears this gold multi color low cut fitted dress, with purple six-inch heels, her makeup and hair is always point.

Keisha wears a white bralette, white skirt with a gold chain around her waist, gold multi color rhinestone six-inch heels, hair cut into a bob and natural look for makeup.

Angel wears this black one piece with a low cut really letting her boobs say hello to the world, two split on each side that goes up her thigh leaving nothing to your imagination, red heel that ties around her leg, makeup and hair done to perfection.

Ladies our limo awaits us in the lobby. We are talking and laughing as we walk through the hotel. Everyone's heads are turning looking at these 3 Gorgeous Black Queens. Our personal driver had the door open for us as we got in and champagne awaits us.

This is about to be an epic night Angel said with excitement. Yes, it is also I purchased us the VIP tickets so we can see the full male packages up close and personal. We had a toast to have nothing but fun this weekend and whatever happens in Vegas stays in Vegas.

We arrived at the nightclub dollar bills ready in hand. Our driver Jonathan opened the door to let us out. Jonathan I will call you when we are ready to leave Keisha said. We skip the line and enter as we hear people whisper, "who are they"? They must be important to skip the line and indeed we were. Tanya found our table while Angel and I went straight to the bar to get drinks. We headed to our table because the show was about to start, and we couldn't miss a thing.

Music is playing. Keisha started to dance, enjoying herself letting her hair completely down. Angel ordered food for everyone and Tanya made sure we had bottles served at our table. Keisha made sure she wasn't the only one on the dance floor as she pulled other women, she didn't know on the dance floor just having a great time.

The host said ladies take your seat the show is about to start, and you won't be disappointed.

Ladies, the first dancer to take the stage is Python.

Keisha, I wonder why they call him Python? Hopefully, he is working with something and easy on the eyes. All the ladies said out loud. Python music started to play as he was walking on to the stage. He came out in his firefighter uniform taking pieces off one at a time. Tanya said he looks familiar; y'all don't remember him. No! We've been drinking since we got here, especially Keisha. Angel said in her tipsy voice. Well, we can figure that out later, Keisha replied. Oh Lord he is the complete package body is on point face is gorgeous and extremely easy on the eye's ladies, so this is worth every penny I spent on the VIP section hopefully the other dancers are just as fine.

Python motion for Keisha to get on stage. Keisha looked back and said he was talking to you Angel.

No! Python walking your way right now.

Come here beautiful, Keisha gets up and walks with him back to the stage; in her mind what he has in store for me.

He whispers in her ear stand still I'm about to lift you up. Okay no problem Keisha said anxiously. Tanya and Angel damn he bench pressing and acting like he was eating her pussy up in the air like that; I need my turn to be soon. Python lays Keisha on the floor as he mind fuck her and say you don't remember me? Keisha responds Am I supposed too, you kinda look familiar. I'm Brandon! From the bar.

Oh, fuck me, Keisha said.

We get up and I sit in the chair as Python does a backflip into my legs giving me the best lap dance, I ever got. Damn your sexy you did say your action is better than your words. If you want me to finish the show, you have my number; Brandon said in a pleasing manner. Better yet Brandon, Room 216 you know the location.

See you soon!

Keisha joins the ladies back at the table. Tanya you was right he did look familiar it was Brandon from the bar. The damn bartender Keisha, they both said. Yes! Ladies I have a special event to attend after we finish enjoying ourselves, if y'all don't mind.

Nope! Go finish Python. Angel said.

I will after we finish having fun and besides wouldn't you or Tanya like to have experience on stage, at least get a lap dance. Keisha told the ladies. Hell yeah! Angel said. Ladies, the next dancer gotta be on the same level if not better than Python because he set the tone.

Ladies, Ladies, grab your seat because it's about to be some Turbulence taking the stage. What kind of ride we're about to see, Tanya said with a smile? Hopefully, we're on a long ride, we don't need no 1-minute man. Turbulence wearing this pilot suit just ready to take flight. His caramel ass is taking his time just like an airplane on the runway before takeoff. I like what I see Angel said proudly come here daddy. Angel couldn't wait; she jumped her ass on the stage and showed him what she was working with.

Turbulence gave Angel the baby oil to rub on his chest as she wasted no time to do so. She put her finger in his mouth, bent down to grab his dick, turned around, then started twerking on him as he stood there. He took control pulling her hair and dry fucking her in the doggy style position. Tanya and Keisha are screaming Yazzzzzzzzzzzzzzzzzzz Bitch give it to him. What happens in Vegas stays in Vegas.

Angel finally makes it back to the table turnt up, bitch he can get it. We see the way you were working him on stage as if they called your name.

Tanya your turn. Angel said. No! not tonight, y'all to turnt maybe tomorrow. Tanya replied. Bitch! It's about fun and no judgement zone living our best life. Keisha said with little disappointment. It's time to call Jonathan to pick us up. Hi Jonathan, the ladies and I are ready to leave. Okay! Ms. Keisha I will be there in 10 minutes.

No! problem we will be waiting outside. That was a great time ladies we must do this again.

By the time we made it outside Jonathan was standing outside the limo waiting on us as we walked up, he politely opened the door. Well ladies I know y'all had a great time the smiles on your faces tells it all.

You will be absolutely correct.

Jonathan, can you take us to the nearest edibles shop and liquor store? If you don't mind. Don't leave, we will be quick.

Yes! Anywhere you ladies want to go I will drive you; Well, we here ladies.

Okay! we won't take long, Tanya said to Jonathan.

Fifteen minutes later we are back on the road heading to our hotel. Keisha you have a meeting with Python soon.

Yeah, I do. I'm somewhat nervous because I have been with Tim for so long and now that I'm not it's different connecting with someone on a sexual level.

Just eat some edible gummy bears and take a shot or two of Patron. You will be fine. Remember this is about you starting over having fun and being free with no strings attached, Tanya said to Keisha.

True! I just need to text Brandon aka Python.

Hey Handsome, the ladies and I will be done with our endeavors soon. I will see you around 2am.

Keisha I was waiting for your text now that I have your number we can communicate outside the bar or club. I will be there, Room 216 at 2am. See you soon Beautiful.

Well ladies it's been fun now it's time for me to freshen up and get myself together for Brandon, I will see you beauties tomorrow. Love y'all. Love you to Keisha, see you tomorrow and get a good night's sleep.

Keisha turns music on to relax her as she lays her sexy bra and thong on the bed, before heading to the shower to freshen up. She made sure the water was warm as she washes from head to toe. After 30 minutes in the shower, she steps out, grabs the towel wrapping around her body, brushes her teeth and gargles with mouthwash.

Keisha sits on the bed putting lotion all over her body while singing along with the song. There's little to leave for Brandon's imagination with just a bra, thong and robe on but this is about to be one hella of a ride. She sprayed her favorite fragrance in the air, while sipping on a glass of champagne awaiting Brandon's arrival.

There's a knock on the door. She slowly walks over to open the door; there he stands this fine piece of chocolate with roses in his hand. Hi Python, I mean Brandon as we both laugh. Hi beautiful the roses are for you as he enters my room; thank you Brandon they are so beautiful. Music is still playing to set the tone and to relax us both because now it's just him and I.

Would you like something to drink

Brandon?

Yes! Do you have any water? If not, I will take some Hennessy.

Okay! I have champagne and water, but you don't look like a champagne kind of guy. Keisha hands Brandon a bottle of water.

Yeah, I really don't like the taste of champagne and thanks for the water. Where are you from Keisha?

I live in Maryland, but work in Washington, DC.

How about you Brandon?

I'm born and raised in Vegas, Sin City. So how long have you been dancing Python?

About 6 years the money is pretty decent, not my life goals though. I see myself owning a construction business. So, you and the girls took a trip to Vegas. How do you like it so far?

It's been great. I will definitely come back.

There's something about you that is

different Keisha as we look into each other's eyes and felt the sexual chemistry. She stood up and dropped her robe seducing him as he started to kiss on her stomach grabbing her by the waist. Her hands rubbing on his head.

Brandon tells her to lay on the bed while he takes off his shirt, he climbs on top of her kissing and touching her from head to toe with loud but soft moans. She sucking on his neck as his dick got harder and her pussy getting soak and wet.

Keisha pulls his pants down as his 10-inch dick awaits her mouth. She wrapped a fruit roll around it and sucked it until it was gone. Damn I wasn't expecting this; Brandon said while moaning.

At this time, we both were naked he picked me up and laid me back on the bed as his dick entered my pussy, the stroke got intense and our moans had gotten louder; the headboard hitting the walls as he went deeper inside.

He flipped her over, hitting it from the back while pulling her hair, kissing on her ear and moving down to her neck, and damn did he smell good. Keisha finally takes control climbing on top riding him as her breast finds a place in his mouth. He pulls her closer to him as they are passionately kissing, Brandon is smacking and grabbing her ass.

Keisha turns around, her ass is in his face as she is still riding to please him, her ass is bouncing all in his face as you hear the wetness of her pussy. Brandon pulls Keisha to the end of the bed; he gets on his knees and starts to eat her honey pot and "Yazzz Lord" he knows what he's doing. He stood up after 10 minutes of pleasing her, slowly putting his dick back in her soaking wet pussy to finish the job.

Her knees were pinned down to her

chest as he jackhammered her pussy. She moans loudly telling him she's about to cum he lifts her up in the air like he was bench pressing her as she climaxes in his mouth. Brandon told Keisha: Lay on your stomach; he just fucking away moaning as he bust his nut on her ass.

We both cleaned ourselves, laid down and watched TV. I must say Brandon you lived up to your name, Keisha said. I told you my actions is better than my words and I must say you fuck me as if I did something to you; you good at what you do. Brandon said with a smile.

As time passed, we both fell asleep with him holding me.

We woke up to the phone ringing and a knock on the door. Opening the door; Keisha, Did Brandon show up? Tell us about last night. Keisha whispers he is still here and shut up y'all loud he can hear you. Do you want us to come back? Hell, yeah come back later Keisha told them.

I guess Brandon somewhat heard them putting his clothes on and walked behind me and said Keisha it's cool I will call you later for dinner and kissed me on the cheek. Good Morning ladies have a good day as he leaves.

Y'all mine as well stay now you interrupted my morning. She takes a quick shower and gets dressed. Okay so are you going to tell us what happened? Well, no not exactly but I will tell you this it was well worth it, and I was pleased in different ways. So, what's on the agenda today let's go ziplining across Fremont. People are giving out fliers with discount coupons. I would love to do something crazy like that while we are here. Ziplining from one end of Fremont to the other end would be a blast. So where are we putting our purses? You better hold it tight.

I'm not leaving my purse with someone I don't know. Good luck with that Tanya tell me how it works out. Just imagine us doing this on day 1. I pray for the people below us because their ass would have been pissed at us nothing but vomit on their heads especially from all the liquor we were drinking.

We need to find something to eat because I'm starving. I barely ate yesterday and then I have a slight hangover. Cheesecake factory is downstairs in the lobby; I don't really feel like going outside. It's way too hot to walk the strip this early.

Keisha, why are you sitting at the table with sunglasses on? Tanya asked. Girl I feel like shit I'm hungover and I'm not a spring chicken once you hit your 30's, liquor hits differently too.

As we are eating Keisha receives a phone call from Tim as she looks at the phone ring. Angel said to Keisha; that's

Tim calling. If you want to talk to him answer the phone, then because I don't. Tim is now texting, "Keisha, Answer the phone." Give me 5 minutes let me call him back as she gets up and walks out the restaurant. Tim, what do you want that's so urgent you're blowing up my phone? I know you're on vacation Keisha, when are you coming back? So, I know if I'm dropping the kids off to school on Monday. Sunday I will be home but you're dropping the kids off at school because I have some early errands to run Monday morning. Ladies, this is our last night in Vegas before it's time to get back to work. I must say I really did enjoy this girl's trip with y'all and there will be one in the next couple of months, Keisha said. To be honest I really needed this to Keisha, Tanya replied. As we waited for Angel to finish up in the restroom. For the rest of the day, I will be relaxing nothing over the top for me, laying by the pool enjoying the beautiful weather and scenery, maybe a drink or two but mostly water. Well Keisha and Angel I'm going back to my room and rest then I will catch back up later on. Okay girly no problem because I'm not too far behind you. We were not staying too long at the pool, probably just for an hour Angel told Tanya.

I always wanted to tell you Angel how proud I am of you and everything you accomplish. You are an intelligent, outspoken, honest, self-motivated young black woman and I can't wait to see what you blossom into, and I really mean it.

Tanya as well I love everything about her how positive she is even through the storm. She's beautiful, determined, trustworthy, uplifting, and has a lot of great things in store for her.

This is why I choose you 2 for the trip because y'all work your butt off and you deserve it.

Come on Keisha this is not the time for me to start crying, what you trying to do here mess up my makeup, give me a hug we both need it. Just in the middle of our crying session Brandon texts; Keisha dinner at 7:00pm if you are still up to it. A smile comes across her face as she texts him back: Yes! sure 7:00pm is fine, which restaurant will I join you at Brandon. I'll pick you up beautiful at 6:30pm. Ok! See you then. It must be Brandon because I know Tim not putting a smile on your face like that. You must like him; Angel asks Keisha in a curious way. Yeah, just a little but nothing serious I'm not ready for that. Besides it's fun for now I live in Maryland and he stays here in Vegas. I just don't see anything happening in a serious way, I can't see myself in a long-distance relationship.

To be honest after everything I went through with Tim, I'm definitely not ready to take the leap of faith on a relationship for a long time. Well Keisha you can't hold back from being loved by the right person based on what Tim did. Yes, he scarred you but don't keep picking at your scars because they won't heal for true love.

You're absolutely right Angel but it's so hard after giving someone all of you and getting nothing back but heartaches, headaches, and mistakes. I love our four children. They are very precious to us and the only thing that went right.

I understand Keisha focuses on you and your kid's happiness and everything else will fall into place, besides, you have this hot sexy man ready to take you out so let's go back to our rooms and you get dressed for a wonderful evening and get your mind off the negativity, only positive vibes allowed.

Thanks! For the talk Angel, I really needed that. Keisha sincerely said.

Anytime, Keisha.

Just in time freshly out the shower and dress when Brandon knocks on the door. You look absolutely gorgeous Keisha; you don't look too bad yourself. So, Brandon where are we going?

We're going to an outstanding 5-star restaurant, which I already reserved a table for us.

Ok! Brandon, I see you.

We walked towards Brandon's Hummer. He opened the passenger side door and helped me in because it was way too high off the ground especially with heels on.

Brandon hops in the driver seat and rolls down the windows to feel the air while playing soft and intimate music. Keisha I would really like to get to know you more beyond our sexual connection if you don't mind. You are different from the other women that I came across and I want to explore.

I really appreciate that, Brandon but

right now, I'm not looking for anything serious at the moment. So, who's the guy that broke your heart the reason you have this wall up. Brandon, I don't want to talk about it, I just want to enjoy us and this evening. Keisha I'm here to listen while holding my hand and his other hand on the steering wheel.

We pull up to the valet. He opens my door. Brandon hands the valet guy the keys, then we walk into the restaurant and wait in line. The hostess asks "How can I help you" with a smile on her face, I have a reservation for 2, Brandon said.

You can follow me to your table and your server will be with you shortly. You're such a gentleman and thanks for pulling my chair out for me. No problem, this is how a real man is supposed to treat a woman, especially one that is deserving of it.

You know what I do for work, tell me

something about you Keisha. Well, I'm a mother of 4 beautiful children, I own a real estate company, educated, understanding, loving, open and honest, trustworthy.

So, are you with your children's father? No! We recently divorce about 9 months ago.

How old are you Keisha?

32.

How about you Brandon?

I'm 30.

How about you single, married, engaged, complicated, entanglement? No, I'm not involved with no one I would love to be married with kids. I will eventually know when I found the right one. I don't mind dating someone with kids as long as she doesn't have a basketball team as we both laugh. Keisha, I really want to see where this goes whether friends or something deeper than that. It's all up to you but I'm open. I know you are not ready for a relationship because of your past and we haven't known each other for only 2 days but I enjoy our conversation. For me as a man I need someone to believe in GOD, she has to be beautiful inside and out, someone who can intellectually stimulate my mind, someone I can build with who has goals that needs to be accomplished and working towards them, someone that has flaws and owns them. For me Keisha you embodied all of them. I don't know what to say Brandon. I enjoy our conversation too and there's an undeniable, unspoken attraction beyond the sexual chemistry. But I'm at the point in my life being in a relationship right now is not the right move for me. I don't want you to get hurt nor myself, we can be friends. Besides, I live in Maryland and I just don't see how a long-distance relationship would work. I agree to a certain point about it being too early for a relationship, but I will tell you this: a real man goes after what he wants and if it's a long-distance relationship, he will make it work especially if the woman is worth it. Just in time our server brought us our food and the drinks we ordered. Brandon gave blessings over our food, which was different because Tim never did that. Keisha stares at Brandon in his eyes trying to figure out if this man is really genuinely being himself or is, he putting on an act.

Question Keisha: Why are you looking at me like that; did I do something wrong?

No not at all just trying to figure out some things that's all. Sorry about that Brandon, staring at someone is rude. I get it we all have our moments, right now is just your moment as he smiles looking her in her eyes.

Brandon's phone rings and he looks at it and doesn't answer. Whoever it is called back, and he still didn't answer. As much as she tries to ignore the fact, he has not answered his phone twice she just couldn't look past it. She has seen this shit before with Tim and refuses to be in the same mess, but as the side chick in his girlfriend's eyes. Brandon, why haven't you answered your phone?

Because it's rude and disrespectful besides it's some chick I used to talk to 2 years ago.

Or do you mean you're currently talking too, I just don't have time for the games, I finished going through this with my ex and I refuse to do it again. No! I'm being 100 percent honest with you, she is an ex from 2 years ago nothing more nothing less. If I had a girlfriend, I definitely wouldn't be here with you. I'm very faithful and committed to the person I'm dating. Keisha drank her champagne yeah okay. Well, it's getting late and I need to pack because tomorrow I leave to go home. Brandon takes care of the check and we proceed to leave.

I notice you have been quiet during the entire ride Keisha. Nothing is wrong Tim; shit I mean Brandon. I didn't mean to call you Tim, it just slipped out. I'm so sorry. Why is Tim so important for you to be calling me his name, when you know my name is Brandon and you're here with me.

I feel like an idiot. Tim is the father of my children and my ex-husband and he is not important in my life that way anymore only for the kids.

You have personal things to sort out because I'm not second best or an afterthought. I'm a grown ass man and need to know if we ever make it beyond friends. I have your mind, body, and soul without any distractions.

I utterly understand how you feel Brandon but again we are just friends. We finally pull up to the front of the hotel. He places the car in park, he gets out the car to open up my door as he helps me out. We are looking at each other as Brandon and I kiss. Thank you for a wonderful evening Brandon.

You're welcome Keisha; talk to you soon.

Keisha heads to her room and texts Tanya and Angel, Ladies I'm back in my room see you in the morning.

Chapter 10

"She needs a Clear Mind"

We all met in the lobby to leave and she couldn't get Brandon off her mind especially calling him Tim. Sorry ladies for not meeting back up yesterday, I needed to relax, Tanya said. We understand but I'm really interested in how Keisha and Brandon date night went, Angel responded.

I just don't want to talk about it. I feel bad for calling him Tim by accident. Girl what the fuck you call him Tim, What the hell is wrong with you? They both said in sequence. I didn't mean it something happened, that triggered me that's all, not getting into details, let's change the conversation.

Ladies, we finally made it home. I'll see

you tomorrow. Keisha enters her empty home ready to relax and catch up on sleep. She calls her mom just to check in to get caught up on conversation before she takes a nap. She pours a glass of wine as she cozy up on the couch watching TV. Six hours later she wakes up not realizing she fell asleep. She hops in the shower and fixes dinner afterward; she still feels tired as she thinks to herself the vacation was fun but damn I did way too much now it's catching up to me.

Chapter 11

"Communication"

Several weeks past Keisha and Brandon still communicate as she still tries to keep her distance, so she won't catch feelings for him. However, they did plan a trip for Brandon to come visit very soon. So far Keisha family and work life has been going so great and she couldn't complain. Keisha's workload has been crazy, clients coming from every angle, showing houses and negotiating contracts. Tanya and Angel are doing a great job as always and matter of fact Angel is recently engaged and expecting a beautiful bundle of joy, I'm so happy for her and her fiancé. Summertime is rolling around and my children are so ready for vacation, Tim and I normally have three vacations for them but unfortunately it will be a little different this time.

Now Tim and I need to discuss how the summer arrangement will be for the children. She really doesn't want to hear his voice, so she texts him instead. Hi Tim, we need to discuss the summer arrangement for the children. I was guessing they would stay with me for one month and a half and you have them the remainder of the summer if you don't mind and put them into summer activities as well.

Keisha so what about our family vacation we normally have I still want to plan something. But besides that, I'm fine with everything else. Tim you're really pushing it. To be honest I'm not up for it but to keep some kind of structure for our children I will ONLY go on one family trip that's it. Let me make this clear we are not getting back together, no touchy feely absolutely nothing.

Ok cool Ladybug I got it.

Kids home from school dropping their bookbags by the front door; they look exhausted. Working so hard to make up any homework they missed and also taking their final test. They really deserve a nice getaway for the summer, especially everything they've been through.

Unknown number constantly keeps calling Keisha's phone, but they won't leave a voicemail or text. When she tries to ignore it, she wonders who it is, they finally call back and she answers.

Hello, who is this?

Hi Keisha, this is Tiffany?

Oh, hell no what do you want. I don't know if you have selective memory or what, but I told you not to call me anymore. Did you not get the message when I didn't respond to the last text you sent me a couple of months ago? I don't want to talk to you, remember. Keisha, I know but I really want to let you know I had my second child and recently had a DNA test done on both of my children to see if they're Tim's or KJ.

I don't care Tiffany you need to be talking to KJ and Tim about the results, I can't get you pregnant so why in the hell would I want to know. Well let me just say this Keisha neither one is Tim nor KJ. I really thought to a certain point KJ jr was Tim child. I'm just so broken down I don't know who my children's father is. I just don't know where to start. How can I explain this to KJ? I really love him and want this to work.

Can I tell you my honest opinion Tiffany, close your legs and go see a therapist and take it to GOD because I can't help you? Goodbye.

This bitch really had the nerve to call me with this bullshit like I wanted to know. I'm trying to move on without any reminders of Tim besides our children. What he did to break up our happy home is no longer my problem nor do I care.

I had other things to worry about like when Angel goes on maternity leave, I will need to find a replacement temporarily. Matter of fact I need to inform my client Mr. Blackwell that his offer was accepted, and he will be able to move in sometime this weekend.

Also call Mr. Stevenson to let him know I'm still going back and forth with the other realtor to come to some kind of agreement, so Mr. Stevenson can move into his home within the next couple of weeks.

Chapter 12

"Girl Talk"

Tanya I'm throwing Angel a surprise baby shower I already spoke with her fiancé and he's fine with it. So, I rented out an event space and hired someone to cater, decorate, DJ, and made sure they had a moon bounce or some kind of activities if someone brings their children. This will be so perfect for her and him. I can't wait to see the smiles on their faces.

Alright Lady, I must say beyond everything that's been going on, I'm much happier and also Brandon and I have been talking and texting on the regular. I'm starting to really like him more than what I thought maybe even more than just friends. It's been more than one year and I'm starting to have strong feelings for him, but I don't want to tell him yet.

I'm not ready to introduce him to my children yet and especially not Tim. But when I eventually introduce him to them and they don't get along that's a deal breaker for me, my children are my everything and I refuse to put a man over top them.

Keisha, I understand that but why does he need to meet Tim? Also, he doesn't seem like the type that would want you to put him over your children.

I thought the same way about Tim he would never cheat in our marriage and have children with different women, but he did, so anything can seem a certain way but actually the opposite just saying Tanya. To answer the first part of your question I would like Brandon to meet Tim not for the approval of Tim but for him to know who's around his children; it's still a level of respect I have for him despite what he has done.

So, I guess when he comes to visit, we will make our mind up whether we are together or not and he will meet Tim. Okay! Keisha just take your time and don't rush or push the issues because you know how Tim is. He can be a firecracker when it comes to his family and yes you are still considered his family.

True I absolutely understand where you're coming from, but Tim can't really speak on who I can and cannot date. He lost that privilege a long time ago. Speaking of him, Tim is calling in on the other line, talk to you later Tanya.

Chapter 13

"Tim's Idea"

Hey Tim, how are you and how can I help you? Why are you talking to me like I'm your client? I wanted to discuss our family vacation as soon as possible so I can book and pay for everything in advance if you don't mind Keisha. I was thinking about getting a penthouse overseas just don't know the location yet.

Well Tim that sounds cute and expensive, let's just keep it simple. We can vacation in Hawaii on a beautiful resort with a penthouse. You have everything you need now, send me the information after you book it. The kids and I will meet you at the airport when it's time.

So, I can't come pick you and the kids up, what kind of shit is that Keisha we still family. Do you realize we will be sleeping in the same penthouse for a week, we need to find a common ground somewhere? Keisha it's been a long two years and some change, and you are still paying me back.

Tim the common ground was when I agreed to this family vacation and to be in the same area as you. Don't push it because I'm not here for it, just send me the details and the kids and I will meet you at the airport. Thanks Tim. Alright Ladybug. Yeah, and that's another thing I'm not your ladybug anymore my name is Keisha to you for now on.

Chapter 14

"Walls Up"

Keisha closing deals left and right. She is so busy, now she only talks to Brandon through text because by the time she gets home she's tired and helping the kids with their homework to fixing dinner. She has tons of things on her plate and she knows Brandon is feeling pushed to the side, and honestly, she doesn't want him to feel like that.

She just wants all her clients to be satisfied with her work and less workflow when she comes back after Angel baby shower, family vacation, and the arrival of Brandon right after. Later that evening Brandon texts: Can you pick up your phone so we can talk.

Yeah, just give me a sec; Brandon I'm just getting out the shower. She really wants to go to bed, but he needs his time, Keisha said to herself.

Brandon calling....

Hi Brandon!

Keisha what's going on, you've been very distant not calling as much. What are we doing, are we together or not? I never felt this way about anyone. My feeling for you is getting stronger. But you steadily pushing me on the back burner as if I did something or am, I paying the price for what your ex did... Brandon, Brandon. Hold on Keisha let me finish first. I'm not your ex I'm more than your ex, but you to blind to see it. Like I told you when you were here in Vegas. I'm all in. I meant that. Is that the problem you and your ex got back together, and you don't know how to tell me huh Keisha? Or you just don't see yourself with a real man that loves you, shit do you even care that I just told you I love you. What do you want from me?

Brandon, I've just been so busy with work and the kids, I just don't have the time to talk on the phone for hours. I don't want you to feel like you're not important to me because you are. Tim and I will never get back together that is completely over. I have strong feelings for you. I can't deny that but is it love I don't know; I just don't want to get my heart broken again. What I need from you is patience, time, and understanding Brandon.

Don't act like I haven't noticed you didn't answer some of my questions. I will need an answer when I come see you, I can't waste my time baby. I can't be the only one all in and I refused to get my heart broken Keisha. Call me when you're available or better yet when I'm worth your time, goodnight. My mind is troubled after talking to Brandon. I understand he's hurt or better, yet he doesn't think I'm considering his feelings, but "what about me"? I gave my all to someone before and received nothing but drama and a divorce. Maybe Brandon is right. I could be paying him back for something he didn't create. But right now, I gotta stay focused on other things. I will talk to him when he comes and visit to clear the air.

Chapter 15

"Keeping Busy"

Next morning, everyone is preparing for what the day brings, kids getting ready for school and I'm heading to work. Good Morning Angel, can you gather everyone for the staff meeting please? Thanks a lot. Hey guys, today we will be discussing sales, clientele and my appreciation for you.

Just to let everyone know GREAT JOB sales have been up by 25% as you know real estate has its moments. Sometimes the housing market is too bad to buy and you have moments like this where everyone is either selling or buying houses, etc.....

When it comes to our clients, they are our #1 priority making sure the offers are sustainable, appraising their homes, etc.... correctly. Going up and beyond but within reason for them. I have a wonderful staff that anyone would want and have working for them, I have noticed what each and every one of you brings and has to offer. Keep up the good work and I really do appreciate you to the fullest.

I still can't get Brandon off my mind and especially after what he said last night. He didn't call or text, maybe I did push him too far and that's not what I wanted. She texted him: Hi Baby, about the conversation last night can we talk about it. Nope! not at all besides I'm busy right now Keisha. Okay talk to you later, she replied.

Brandon just brushed me off; how could he, I didn't deserve that. I definitely will talk to him about that, completely unnecessary. Well, it's time to wrap up for work and head home. During the drive home she wanted to call him but never picked up the phone, maybe he needs more time to process our conversation and how he just brushes me off. Finally made it home to my relaxing bed and prepared dinner then off to bed I went.

Chapter 16

"Angel's Baby shower"

Several days later, it's time for Angel's surprise baby shower. Tanya and I arrive 3 hours early to make sure everything is perfect. I made sure she will never forget her special day. Tons of different color balloons, king and queen chairs for her and her fiancé, custom made baby backdrop with her name and picture, lavish diaper cake, cupcake cake with fondant saying am I a boy or girl, stars hanging from the ceiling, a gift table decorated with baby toys, other tables decorated with blue or pink (you had to seat at the blue or pink table based on what you thought Angel was having), moon bounce outside, popcorn and cotton candy stand, etc....

Anything you could think of was there. Her fiancé texted me and said they're outside. He placed a blindfold over her eyes and of course she wasn't having it for too long. Keisha yells they are here, everyone finds a place to hide, lights are off, no one is making a sound. We see the door open and the sunlight shines as Angel asks her fiancé what are you doing and why do I have a blindfold on.

He said baby we are almost there just two more steps and I will take it off. Okay Angel said anxiously. He took it off, everyone yelled "this is all for you and your fiancé Angel congratulations". As Angel places her hands over her face tears are falling down this is all for us, I can't believe it. I never had someone do something special like this for me.

She looks at her fiancé. You knew about this as he answered yes, your boss Keisha called me because she wanted to do something incredibly special. Her eyes and the words that came out of Angel's mouth I knew right there she was thankful, and mind blown on how beautiful this turned out for them. Keisha you really fool me, and you never spoke a word at work nor did Tanya y'all are something else and at least I know y'all can keep a secret as we laugh. Love you Angel and you deserve it to the fullest your bundle of joy is something to celebrate. Thank you Keisha and Tanya I really do appreciate it.

Chapter 17

"Open and Honest for New Love"

After everyone left the baby shower Tanya and I stayed to clean up with the vendors. I must say we absolutely outdid ourselves. Angel looked beautiful as always and her fiancé is a gentleman, Tanya said. I'm so ready to go home and relax on the couch. Driving home Keisha calls Brandon's phone ringing about 4 times already, hopefully he picks it up. Hello, who is this? Brandon asked. What do you mean? Who is this? You forgot about me already, what kind of bullshit is this. That's exactly why I didn't want to get too close to you. You already moved on so quickly you don't even know who you speaking to. Fuck you; I can't with this shit.

Keisha what you tripping for I thought this is what you wanted from me to act like I don't care. What the hell do you want me to do because when I care you put me on the back burner, I love you for real not playing any games with my heart I'm too old and too grown to be trying to figure out what's the next step. Everything is up to you; this relationship will be how you make it. Brandon, there's not a day that goes by that I don't think about you.

This is not what I wanted. I know my actions are quite different from my words, but I needed time. The conversation we last spoke was an eye opener for me because you were right. A part of me was making you pay for what Tim did and that's not right at all. I'm sorry that I made you feel any type of way my past is not your fault. I want us to be together and see where it goes with no distraction. I'm all in.

Can you forgive me Brandon?

Keisha, I already did forgive you. I knew where the push back was coming from. I know how harsh us men could be and the damage we can cause to someone that meant everything to us. I'm not faulting you on your feelings, you needed to take your time and work things out at your own pace. I just refuse to put my heart into something to get it broken because you were unsure.

I'm glad you understood most men don't. I also wanted to tell you this Tim and I will be taking the children on a week vacation very soon right before you come down to visit. Didn't want you to be caught off guard, it's only for the children.

You are a grown ass woman I can't tell you not do something I'm not your father nor am I looking to be. I trust you and your word, that's it just for the kids' sake nothing more or less.

Thanks for informing me though. I can't wait to see you. It's been an exceedingly long couple of months. For real I need to tell you something in person that's important to me. Okay so you just not going to tell me, why do I need to wait until I see you if it's important. I needed to make sure you were the right one for me before I disclose this particular thing about me. When I would let certain people, I dated know they changed and act like I owed them something. I needed to find a special person I felt connected with, understood and wasn't looking for a come up nor a bank account with countless withdrawals, but the only thing they brought was insufficient funds.

It seems to me that you dated a lot of girls that consider themselves a woman because of their age but let me tell you this; I'm grown woman I have my own money I absolutely work extremely hard for and I would never use anyone for anything that's very grimy, disrespectful, dishonest, no self-respect, and totally unacceptable at all cost. I'm a different kind of woman if we don't have something, we will build together to make sure we do have.

I knew it was something different about you, I appreciate it. I'm glad we had this conversation. How is everything going besides us? My workload has been crazy and constantly busy. I can barely take a lunch break. I have a wonderful staff in which I just threw this elegant over the top baby shower for my receptionist Angel, my children are doing very well with the last week in school and grades are on point.

My mom is also doing well besides that there's nothing else. Baby I'll call you tomorrow it's been an exceedingly long work week. Okay! Baby love you.

Brandon said. Love you too, Keisha

responded.

After getting off the phone "Did I really say I love you? It rolled off my tongue so smooth, I know this feeling all too well. Butterflies start, blushing when I hear his voice, can't wait until he calls or text me, or better yet waiting for him to come home.

Chapter 18

"Family Vacation"

Next couple of weeks has past school have ended for the children, time for the family vacation. Tim finally sent over all the information, we flew first class which is great and more room heading to Hawaii. Can't wait to just relax and clear my mind and enjoy my children, while talking to Brandon here and there. As much as I really want to act like Tim is not there I can't and even if I did, he would make his presence known.

The kids and I met him at BWI Airport at 6am tired as hell but the kids were excited to see their father and go to Hawaii. Tim checked everyone luggage in as we proceeded through security lord knows how long security can take especially when you have kids it seems longer. Finally made it through the security checkpoint, kids were hungry, so Tim and the boys went to grab something to eat from a different restaurant from my daughter and I, we just met back up at a common location.

We all sitting down eating Keisha sits across from Tim as she is not really trying to make eye contact or talk to him. Here we go Keisha. We really need this vacation and you deserved it after everything. Tim, not right here do we need to have this conversation. But you are absolutely right we all need the beautiful vacation enjoying the beach and nice weather.

Our youngest son Alim asked Tim, Daddy are we getting on a plane and flying in the sky like birds? Tim laughs. Yes! Son we are flying like birds.

The cutest moment so far and to a

great start Keisha thought to herself. Time to take a restroom break before our plane starts to board in 20 minutes and everyone knows how much I hate using the plane restroom. Once everyone was finished with the restroom, we headed towards our gate number to board the plane and since we had children, we boarded first on the plane besides seniors and people with disabilities.

My three oldest sat in front of Tim, Alim and myself. I kinda wish Tim would have switched seats with one of the kids but oh well it's not about me. Keisha, I know we are only co-parenting, but I miss you dearly. I'm glad you understood we are only co-parenting, but Tim's time has passed so has the feelings. Also, I told you Tim this is about our children and their happiness we will not make this vacation about us. You right Ladybug I just had a moment my bad.

She knew this would be a long vacation, just when the flight attendant walked by, she ordered an alcohol beverage to finish the rest of the flight. Keisha what's wrong you don't normally have a drink when the kids are around. Nothing Tim, I'm fine. So, we staying in a penthouse that has 4 bedrooms, 2 bathrooms, an enormous kitchen, a balcony with a gorgeous view of the ocean, butler, etc.... To make you feel comfortable Keisha you have your own room. Thanks Tim I really appreciate it. Our daughter Johnaya turns around and asks, "How long do we have"? Soon as we were about to answer the pilot came on the intercom: Hello everyone we will land in 45 minutes, sunny weather in Hawaii is 85 degrees, we are enjoying your company and thank you for flying with us. My oldest son is so impatient he's just ready to get off, the other two kids asleep.

Keisha catches herself staring at Tim as she quickly snaps back in reality, he looks really good. We made it to paradise Tim holding Alim while we walked to baggage claim. Tim on the phone with someone letting them know we are here. Our limo is pulling up in 10 minutes, so we need to make sure we have all our suitcases.

Tim you didn't need to rent a limo you could have booked a super shuttle Keisha said. Nah my family receive luxury and nothing but the best, besides if I were to book a super shuttle that's for friends with benefits kind of females. Some things don't never change looking at Tim. Brandon is calling Keisha while she is in the limo. Hi Baby, "You off of work"? Keisha said with a smile. Yeah, I'm just checking on you "Did y'all make it yet"? We just landed now in the limo going to the resort. Okay cool have fun we can text throughout the time you are there, not

trying to interrupt your family
vacation. Okay but I will call you when
the kids go to sleep. Alright Baby Love
you, love you too Keisha said back.

She can feel Tim's eyes staring at her
while the hair on her neck is standing
up. Who was the homeboy you were
telling you love him? You lost your
privilege to ask me any questions about
my love life. We can talk about it later
when the kids go to sleep Tim said
since you'll have time to talk to dude
with no name. Tim not today I don't
have time for your bullshit.

Keisha looks out the window taking in
the beautiful scenery, as the wind
bushes her chocolate face inhaling the
air and exhaling with a smile on her
face. We arrived at the resort with
people greeting us with the cutest
Hawaiian dance and placing a necklace
of flowers (Lei) around our necks.

Tim checked us in while the children
and I walked around looking at the

different pictures and statues, picking up pamphlets of different activities they have. Tim met up with us while the concierge brought our bags to the room. Let's go freshen up before we enjoy the beach Tim said. Yeah, the flight seems like it took forever so we definitely need to freshen use the restroom and make sure our bags made it to our room.

Tim gave the room key to our daughter for some reason she loves hotels, resort anything that is the opposite of home. Johnaya opens the door and places her hands over her mouth. Are you serious? We can live here. This thing is huge. Our sons of course are not as animated as our daughter; they just look at her; it's just a different resort and different location.

Keisha was taken back to how enormous, beautiful, breath taking the view is, as she says to Tim I really gotta hand it to you; you really outdid yourself this time. The way I envision the penthouse after you describe it to me is way better in person.

Told you I can't let my family down this is for us Tim said with a smile on his face. To be honest Tim next time used a better choice of words "can't let the family down" hmmm you did that already, Keisha responded. For real you knew what I meant ladybug, come on now this is about fun and family time. Let's go enjoy this nice weather and get some food, everyone dress in their swimwear ready to go. We tried their buffet that has an assortment of different foods and desserts. Some food I didn't want to touch, and the other selection was fairly good. After lunch, the beach scene here we come water crystal blue, sea turtle and a variety of fishes swimming. Keisha and the children feeding the sea turtles bananas while Tim takes pictures.

Laughing splashing water really

enjoying each other's time including Tim. Tim stands by Keisha in the ocean watching the kids having fun, while they have small talk. We did a phenomenal job raising 4 intelligent, bright, open minded, beautiful children I must say myself Keisha. Yeah, we did. Just to let you know your boy toy called while I was taking pictures, I politely press the end button. What the fuck Tim why would you do that I ask you to only take pictures with my phone not to screen who calls or text me. Also, Brandon is not my boy toy he is my man the one I love, and you will not come between that.

Keisha I wasn't screening your call. I just thought he wasn't important enough to tell you or better yet important enough to interrupt the picture I was taking of my family; what do you mean you love him? How do you know it's not lust, and you truly still love me while looking in Keisha's eyes?

I'll give you some time to think about your answer while I partake in this Don Julio. Kids swimming towards us Tim we will continue this conversation later on tonight.

Laying on the beach chairs, kids and Tim playing volleyball. I finally get a break to call Brandon back. Hi baby, are you enjoying yourself? Brandon asked.

Yeah, I am. I wanted to say sorry I just saw that you called. I miss you and in two weeks it will be you and I enjoying each other's company. True I can't wait either. It's been way too long since I held you. How are the kids? They just came out of the water now playing volleyball with their dad.

Tim looked at Keisha as she's on the phone with a smile on his face. Okay I'm glad everyone is having fun; Brandon said. Yeah, I can't complain I'm loving every minute of it seeing them bond with their dad its really refreshing.

Alright Babe I'm not going to hold you up, love you just text me later. Love you too. Right before I can hang up Tim yells love you too. Keisha, I heard your ex-husband he's funny call or text me later baby.

Time to go in before we all get sunburns besides, we need to relax, bathe again and go to dinner later on. Yeah, I will make reservations for this restaurant they have at the resort, Tim said.

Later that evening Tim and I finally were able to continue our conversation from earlier and of course we have some alcohol beverages relaxing on the balcony. I would like to answer the question you asked me earlier; Yes! I will always love you Tim. How could I not you are the father of our children? I spent a great part of my life with you. However, that is where it stops at co-parenting.

But about me loving Brandon, a part of me didn't believe I loved him at first because I was still wrapped up in what happened between you and I. But as time went on the way he treated me like a queen. He's understanding, supportive, he constantly expresses his feelings towards me. I had to let down my wall and accept him in and kick you out.

There's not a day goes by that I don't think of Brandon, every time I hear his voice my heart skips a beat, I get goose bumps, I don't want us to get off the phone. We are n'sync we complete each other's sentences. I look at my phone just to see if I missed his call or text. He is an upstanding guy that I could ever ask for, he sees my flaws as beauty marks leading me to happiness because I already survive the storm.

Our foundation is based on honesty, no judgement and that's what I needed. I love him Tim and right now Brandon is who I see myself with. I respect and I understand it. I let a great woman go and emotionally fuck you up I own everything I did or said, I really had time to think about how selfish I was. You deserve happiness even if it's not from me but I'm always here for you no matter what.

How long have you been dating what his name? Brandon, Tim come on now Keisha replied as Tim laughed you know I've been drinking. Have the kids met him and when will I meet him if he's going to be spending time with them. What does Mr. Brandon do for a living?

I think it's too early for him to meet our children and I prefer for him to meet you first and that will be in two weeks from today. Also, he works as a male exotic entertainer and bartender.

We have been dating for about a year or so. Tim spits his Hennessy out and says,'' What a stripper'' Keisha did you lose your damn mind or are you going through a midlife crisis. Hell, nah he's not coming around my children.

Where did you meet him at? I met him in Vegas, and you can't tell me who can be around the kids. Why the fuck I can't they are our kids together. He can't even support himself. I know he can't support you and the kids come on ladybug I know I fucked up, but you completely downgraded.

Shut the fuck up Tim I'm not with him because of his money remember I married a man that didn't have shit and we build our empires now he owns one of the top landscaping business in the world I believe that's you Tim and you still an asshole with money now.

True but I supported our family and still is. Your money is still in your bank account and I'm paying all your bills and whatever the kids need, and their bank accounts are on point, so you don't want for nothing. Tim don't do that; you know damn well I can support myself and children with no problem.

Keisha, I know you can take care of the bills, but he can't. So, Brandon is going to live off of you? I can't see me letting that happen not after we works so hard to make shit happen and then I'm still paying for everything, fuck no another grown ass man is not living off me.

Tim, I understand but you taking this to far Brandon is staying in Vegas nor are we moving in together that quickly the well-being of our children comes first. Brandon has ambition, dreams that he wants to accomplish, and I will help him along the way to make sure it happens.

Tim I would rather drop the conversation, hell you lucky I'm talking to you period. Why are you getting so sensitive about playboy? Huh Keisha if that's what you want, I will drop the conversation.

Keisha, I need you to help me find a house I was meaning to ask a long time ago, but you weren't trying to talk so.... Why you can't stay where you are and there are so many different real estate brokers and companies you can choose from.

Why me? Come on ladybug why not you. I trust your judgement and besides it's a win win for both of us, I get a house and you commission. This is strictly business Tim, what are you looking for six bedrooms, four bathrooms, and down the street from you etc..... similar to the one we own now Keisha. You are not moving close to me and I don't want to see you every time I open my door, you need to put the henny down because you're tripping now.

Keisha remember when we first met, we used to joke about how I couldn't afford to buy you a 50-cent snicker back in the day. Yeah, I definitely remember; til this day it's one of our funny moments we share. I miss those days when it was you and I against the world, I know what you are about to say yeah yeah, it's over, but I cherish each moment, we started with nothing and made something with our lives, and I thank you for that.

Can't no one replace you I will always have your back no matter who I'm dealing with she will need to jump on board or get the fuck off, my family always is number one. I really appreciate it Tim and cherish every moment as well but drinking henny has you very in touch with your feelings. It's not the liquor. I really feel like this. Where the fuck was this person in our marriage I can't with you right now. Keisha stands up looking at Tim. I'm going to bed, hold on ladybug, what Tim, I'm still in love with you as he stands in front of her with a seductive look in his eyes he leans in for a kiss. She pushes Tim back, what are you doing? I'm with Brandon, yeah, I know Keisha but you here with me right now. No! Tim you had too much to drink I'm blaming it on that. She opened the balcony door and headed to her room. She laying on her bed. I know this didn't just happen. The man I was asking and looking for in our marriage all of a sudden wants to appear now. I can't fall for his bullshit.

Hi Python, lol, just wanted to say I love you. Love you too babe goodnight.

Tim knows I'm in a committed relationship how could he. He knocks on the door, Keisha. I'm sorry I know what the deal is just let me in. Tim the door is unlocked. He walks in, sits on the bed my bad. I cross the lines I should've respect your relationship with playboy.

I expect this from you. You want what you want, this has always been you Tim.

I want you, but I can't have you right so that statement isn't true. Why are you trying to fight it? You feel the same way right now Keisha I can see it in your eyes; mane man doesn't need to know shit. Tim climbed on top of her and they started to kiss and touch. Tim you right I do want you right now, but I can't have this on my conscience. I know how it feels being cheated on, I never cheated on you and I won't start with Brandon.

Tim you gotta go to your room. For real Keisha, my man woke up and you're just going to send me to my room it's cool tho. Goodnight ladybug love you. Goodnight Tim.

Four days later the kids are still having a blast. Tim planned for us to swim with the dolphins today, we never thought about that one something different so excited. We could see from the outside there was a dolphin show being performed. Jack the dolphin doing all sorts of tricks jumping in and out the water, waving his fin, talking in dolphin (lol). Amy the trainer is who we met up with after the show to have our private swim session with Jack the dolphin, all the kids were on board to feed Jack except for Elliott he wasn't having it.

Amy provides great information about Jack, how smart, intelligent and how he loves people, especially children. Amy asks who wants to swim with Jack, Tim jumps straight in the water and yells I'll go first. Amy instructed Tim to relax, hold on to Jack fin and he will guide you under water and bring you back up.

If you let go, Jack will come back for you. They can sense if someone is drowning or need help. Keisha and the kids passed on the swim except for

Khalif. This is once in a lifetime holy moldy. This is awesome and scary at the same time, but I enjoyed it.

After Tim and Khalif changed their clothes it was time to shop at the stores located on the resort. Buying some souvenirs, swimwear, glasses, hats, etc..... Daddy, when is the next family vacation? Johnaya asked. Baby girl we have not finished with this one yet, how about this we can plan one when you and your brothers stay with me during the summer break. Okay! Because I have some great ideas, maybe we go to Spain, Dominican Republic, that's just to name a few.

I hear you baby girl you have expensive taste and stay in my pockets. Yup I sure do daddy can you buy me these sunglasses, soda and chips, thanks. Yes, I got it. Keisha looks at Tim you created the diva in her as she laughs. My boys are so simple compared to my daughter she needs her fingernails polish, hair done, clothes and purses to match her shoes. Tim said. Sorry to tell you Tim when she gets older it gets worse.

I notice you have been on your phone with Brandon a lot today. Yeah, I have been just planning for him to come down and visit. There's a lot of things Brandon and I need to discuss in person moving forward with our relationship.

Besides that, just checking on Tanya and Angel to see how everything is going at work. I really didn't need you to explain yourself Ladybug. I understand you need to talk to him so he can feel secure. Whatever Tim he's not insecure. In fact, he's confident and handsome, I must say.

Keisha about last night. There's no need to speak. I already let it go, you were drunk Tim. I wasn't apologizing for what I said, those were my honest feelings but for putting you in a position to choose. We are not continuing the bullshit from yesterday. I refuse, I already chose who I want and it's not you. You had a good thing now that I'm gone you want to come back. I'm walking to the room and clearing my head, Tim said. Keisha I can take the kids if you want. Nope! you can go head and clear your head the kids and I will be at the pool. Keisha calls her mom Victoria. Hi mom, I just need someone to talk to. Tim confesses he is still in love with me, but I love Brandon. I finally moved on and here he comes with some bullshit, Tim always was a good guy, but he couldn't keep his dick in his pants and to be honest I don't want to go back to that. Brandon is the opposite of Tim, he's very faithful, not self-centered, understanding and actually listens to me.

But on the flip side of that I love to see my family together and having fun.

Well Keisha you answer your own question. It's time for you to move on with Brandon, besides Tim will always love you, you were married to him and have four children. However, some things aren't meant to be. Where is Tim and the kids? Tim went back to the room and the kids and I went to the pool. It takes men and women different time frames to heal from a relationship Tim is not at that point yet unfortunately. Thanks mom, I really needed this talk. I will call you later. Okay love you, love you to mom and tell Mashaya (Keisha's niece) I said Hi.

She knew she had to call Brandon, hi babe nice to hear your voice, "How is the trip going?" That's what I wanted to talk to you about a couple of days ago. Tim let me know how he is still in love with me and he wants his family back. I told him I was with you but it kinda went to a different level. He kissed me. I did push him away. It was a lot of drinking involved. I'm so sorry baby I didn't mean for that to happen. What the hell you mean he kissed you, what the fuck else y'all do and don't tell me nothing Keisha I'm a fucking man I know how we think. And just when I thought I could trust you; you turn around and do this shit to me. Did you bump your fucking head or what? How the fuck are we supposed to get pass this you just crush me for real. Baby nothing else happen I'm sorry I didn't want you to feel like this at all. You didn't want me to feel like this but yet you still kiss his punk ass back but okay I must be stupid Keisha. Do I have fucking stupid written on my motherfucking forehead. I'm staying faithful to you; how do I know that Brandon. You really have the nerve because my dick stays in my pants my eyes don't wander and lips don't touch no other bitches and if I did cheat right now, I would shove that shit in your face, but I'm too faithful and honest for that bullshit. I want you Brandon not him that's why I'm telling you, I love you not him. Yeah, whatever I'll talk to you later. Brandon, I love then she hears if you like to make a call please hang up and try again.

For the next hour Keisha constantly texting and calling Brandon without an answer. To get her mind off Brandon and the fact she just made a huge mistake by telling him even though it was the upstanding thing to do, she felt like shit. I'm going to let my hair down and enjoy this nice water splashing the kids engaging in water aerobics and just make the most of my time here before we leave in a couple of days. She takes pictures and records the children laughing and dancing, swimming doing cannonballs into the water. Tim finally made his appearance again, to join us. How you feel Tim are you okay now that you had time to yourself. I could be better but what can I do about it? I see the kids having fun. You didn't get in the water? Yeah, I did but I wanted to keep my eyes on the kids. Let's move forward without the tension between us and we could handle whatever we have on our mind later can we agree on that Keisha.

Yeah, I can do that.

Later that night after we all ate and shower, we all watched a movie with snacks of course, just having a wonderful time. Someone's phone is vibrating. Tim gets up and goes on the balcony talking loudly. I told you I was on vacation with my family, don't interrupt me; what part you didn't understand.

I don't want to be with you just because we have a son together doesn't mean I want you; besides how do I know he's my son? I have been asking you for a DNA test and you refuse. But yet I'm taking care of him, he doesn't want for nothing. You're just mad because I'm no longer falling for your bullshit and just handing you money. Don't call me unless it has something to do with our son bye.

He comes back in upset, walks in the kitchen, pours a drink, sits and continues watching the movie. Keisha didn't say not one word and acted like she didn't hear anything. Once the movie was over children went to bed. Keisha walked to her room to settle in. Keisha, can you have a drink with me before you go to bed. Tim you know things get out of hand when you drink. Come on I really need you to have a drink I'm just going through shit right now. Yeah, Tim just one drink after that I'm going to bed. Okay no problem I don't know what to do.

I'm going in circles trying to take care of a child that I don't think is mine, she constantly wants money. She drives me up a wall, only time I can see my son if I bring money or want to get back together and neither one, I'm going to continue doing. This is some bullshit. Well not to kick you while you down but this is what you get when you mess around cheating on your wife with females that's low down. You laid down with dog shit and get up with fleas. I tried to tell you. You thought the grass was greener on the other side now you itching and can't find the correct medication to cure it just saying. But if you really don't think he's your son request a paternity test through the courts, she has no choice but to show up. Which baby mama is this? You know what hold that thought my phone ringing. Hi baby, did you get my text messages? I'm sorry. Yeah, I got 'em what you doing we need to talk, Brandon said. Why are you still up? I'm talking to Tim and having one drink. Okay cool so you are still going to disrespect me by drinking with him for real. That's what the fuck we doing. "Where are the kids"? Sleep, Brandon. I'm not doing nothing; he's just venting about what he's going through. Fuck that; what about what we going through he had his moment to make shit right with you and he chose otherwise, so why are you entertaining his bullshit you still have feelings for him.

No! not in that way I told you that. Did you sleep with him the other night? What the fuck do you mean did I sleep with him hell no, to the fuck nah. Tim in the background laughing did we sleep together what kind of insecure bullshit is that. Shut the fuck up Tim. Don't pay him any attention, he's just an asshole especially when he drinks.

I told you I'm all in but I'm not about to be your fool Keisha. Damn Brandon I love you and want you how many times can I say it. Love you too but you gotta handle that situation with your ex asap I need to stay out of trouble not be in it. When you come back home? In two days. I will certainly talk to him. No, you need to talk to him before I do. Okay I heard you. I have work in the morning Goodnight baby, goodnight.

Back to you Tim which baby mama is it? Man, it's Brittany. I can't stand her ass. With KJ jr. and the newborn baby I supported them too recently Tiffany and I took a paternity test for both children. I haven't received the results back yet. Have you talked to KJ since the cookout? Nope there is no reason too.

Well just to let you know Tim, Tiffany called me weeks ago about the DNA results neither one of the kids is your nor KJ. you might want to call him because you know she didn't tell him, hell, she didn't tell you. What!!!!! say that shit again you gotta be fucking kidding me I'm about to call her.

You can't be mad at her for being the trifling gutter rat she is, blame yourself as well; Keisha laughing so hard you soooo stupid Tim. Maybe next time you will think about who you are sticking your dick in. Keisha that shit isn't funny so they trying to trap me with these damn kids.

Tim calls Tiffany so when was you going to tell me neither child is mines you stupid bitch. I was taking care of these damn kids and you knew they weren't mine, how low can you get. First of all, you put yourself in this situation by cheating on Keisha and you knew I was married to KJ, so the question is how low can you get. Besides, I thought you knew I received my results a while ago. You think if I knew I would be just calling you now how stupid can you fucking be.

Me supporting your kids is cut off I

don't give a fuck what they need or want, find your real baby daddy. Tim, I don't give two fucks I have bigger things to worry about. Yeah, I bet the first thing you need to do is focus on closing your legs then you wouldn't need to be on the Maury show testing multiple guys trying to figure out who's the father. Fuck you Tim get of my phone bastard Tiffany hangs up. That's one for the books. I'm going to sleep, goodnight Tim.

Chapter 19

"According to Our Plans"

Two days later, we made it home safe
and sound and back to reality we go.
Today will be a nice chill day of
relaxing taking a hot bubble bath with
candles lit around the tub soft music
playing and sip on my wine.
Keisha washes her body while thinking
about how Brandon will please her as
her left hand caresses her breast while
she slides her right hand down to her
pussy to pleasure herself soft moans
come out as she climaxes.
She steps out the tub reaching for her
towel to wrap around her, I need
Brandon now reaching for her phone to
call him. She facetimes him baby. I
need you now as she lotions her body.

It has been way too long. I need you inside me and pleasing me in more ways than one.

Ke (Brandon's nickname for Keisha) you know I'm still mad at you. Next week I will be there to break your back in. We will certainly make up for all the months we didn't see each other so be prepared. Every place in the house will be touched with your ass in the air and my dick sliding in and out your pussy. Damnnnn I can't wait as she bites her bottom lip.

Baby I booked the flight and rented a car. Why would you rent a car and waste money, you know I have a car? Yeah, I know that, but I can't depend on your car, what I mean by that is when I come out there as a man, I suppose to make sure I have the necessities to get me from A to B and don't assume we just driving your car everywhere.

You know me, I don't like to take or

live off any woman and especially my girl. Whatever makes you feel comfortable babe. We have a lot to talk about when I get there to make sure we are on the same page and there's no blurred lines. Yeah, I know Brandon, call you tomorrow love you, love you too baby.

Chapter 20

"House Searches"

Tim comes by my office tomorrow before 4:00pm so we can get the process rolling for your house, Keisha text. Morning comes and Keisha gets ready for work. Her mom Victoria comes to stay with the children while she's at work.

She arrived at work. Good morning ladies is everything on point with clients, open houses, etc.... Girl you know we are holding you down boss lady. I know Angel just making sure our clients come first. Did you have a nice vacation with Brandon and where did y'all go? Angel I didn't go on vacation with Brandon.

It was Tim for our yearly family

vacation in Hawaii. Tanya comes out of her office. Did I hear you correctly Tim how did that go? Well, it went good especially when the kids were around, we handled the situation like adults and matter of fact Tim is coming by so I can find him a house, so let me know when he gets here. Soooooo what happened to Brandon? Nothing happened, Brandon coming next week. Ladies we have five minutes before we need to get to work as she walks into her office with her coffee in hand. Tanya did you hear Ms. Boss lady say she and Tim were on vacation? I wonder what happened, I guess we will see when Tim comes, he probably has a big ass smile on his face. Angel you are a hot ass mess and stay out of their business, besides, she is not going to tell you anyway. True true you right I guess I will listen closely when they talking about houses and see if I can catch something.

I just don't know how we deal with you Angel. Because y'all love me Tanya. Couple hours went by with some of my real estate agents hosting open houses, closing deals. Angel calls Ms. Keisha on the intercom. Mr. Jones is in the waiting area do you want me to send him back, yes send him in. Hey Tim let's get down to business I know we discuss some of the information, but we never discuss price range and what you actually looking for besides the bedrooms and bathrooms.

Well okay let me say: Hi Keisha, I need at least five or six bedrooms and four bathrooms, movie room, finish basement, gourmet kitchen, open floor plan, pool, two car garage, basketball court inside the house move in ready. My price range is open but within reason I need everything I just ask for, oh don't let me forget in the same neighborhood as you need to be closer to my kids.

Yeah, I heard you there is no guarantee that everything you are looking for will be available in one house you may need to give and take. Besides Tim do you think five or six bedrooms is enough? You technically have 5 kids plus you. Yeah, Keisha the bedrooms are fine, and I only have four kids and a possible since Tiffany kids aren't mine.

You seriously sitting here talking like you playing spade I have 4 and possible, get your shit together Tim. I will contact some local real estate agents to see what I can get my hands on. Alright ladybug no pressure but I need to move in within the next 3 months or so; my lease is up soon. Oh, another thing since we are here face to face kids coming over this week or next to stay the summer. Uh next week is better for me. I will have more free time and Brandon is coming over. Okay no problem. Playboy coming over with a smirk on his face yeah okay I gotta go. Call you sometime this week to get an update on everything ladybug. Nice doing business with you Tim; likewise, Keisha.

Tanya, did you see Tim? He looked real relaxed compared to when I saw him last time he came to the office. Angel stay out of their business, focus on your pregnancy and fiancé, but I will agree he did look relaxed with a smile on his face. Keisha catches them talking, "What y'all talking about ladies"? Nothing at all Boss lady you and Tim looks relaxed as Angel mumbles. I heard you Angel, Tim and I are in a great place. That's it and that's all drop the topic. I need everyone to make sure all work for today is completed Angel can you let everyone know please. Yeah Keisha, I told her to mind the business that pays her. It's fine Tanya she's just the annoying little sister nobody wanted so we stuck with her as they both burst out laughing.

Chapter 21

"Brandon's Arrival"

Time for Tim to come over and get the children for the summer and while he's here we can discuss the details on the houses. I'm so excited my baby is coming and haven't seen him in months.

Music is playing, she is cleaning the house, doing laundry, making sure everything is in order. Baby I'm tired as hell. I just went through the security checkpoint, so I grabbed something to eat.

This 5-hour flight seems like it will take forever because of the different time zones, I know for sure my sleeping pattern will be off entirely. Baby Maryland time is what 3 hours ahead of Vegas right. Yes, I think so I know my sleep was off for 2 weeks after leaving Vegas.

I just can't wait until you get here, I miss kissing you, we have a lot of catching up to do, especially sex. You know that I am ready to break your back in take all 10 inches. Hold on Brandon, Tim knocking on the door he's picking up the kids. She opens the door; Hey Ladybug, Where the kids? Upstairs packing their things, if they leave or need anything let me know so I can bring it over to them. Nah they should be fine and if not, I will buy it. Sorry baby is your plane boarding yet? Yeah, they haven't called my group yet. Keisha any updates on the houses yet? Tim, can you hold on I will talk to you after I get off the phone. What houses Keisha? I was helping Tim find a new house. Oh, my bad Ladybug I didn't notice you on the phone with playboy I can wait. Tim go see if your kids is ready you've been here too long.

So Ke when was you going to inform me? I wasn't because it's business not personal also some things should just stay between Tim and me. What the fuck, why do he need to know you finding me a house. He's not finding my house nor is he a real estate agent, you know what I'm walking off. Tim shut the hell up for real you starting to get on my nerves.

Baby I'm trying to be respectful, but homie don't have too many more chances with me. I'm letting you know up front I'm not here for the games or bullshit, my group is being called. I will call when I land love you, love you too. Tim why you always gotta show your ass. You are not messing this up for me. I didn't interfere with you and your side bitches oh I forgot I didn't know you were cheating. Don't bring that bullshit up Keisha you know "gooden well" he is not me and will never be me

and he is not good enough for you; stop
playing.

One thing you right on Brandon is not
you I couldn't dare date another you.
Let us change the subject, kids coming,
Tim I looked at several different houses
and most of them didn't come with a
pool but did have acres so you can build
a swimming pool if need be. What are
the price ranges for the houses and
how close are they to you and the kids?
Price starts at 1.2 million up to 2.4
million (negotiable) and 15-30 minutes
away.

Can you send me some pictures over
and I will narrow down the houses I
want to see? Yup no problem but if you
want to move soon, we can't wait too
long. I understand this will be all cash
offers and closing in 10 days, I'm
looking for someone that is eager to sell
their home Keisha. I got you Tim. Y'all
ready to go; Do you have everything?
Yes! Daddy alright let's go. Love y'all,

love you to mommy, love you too ladybug, bye Tim.

She jumps in the shower, brushes her teeth and slips into something comfortable, straightens her hair and puts on some lipstick. Keisha pours a glass of water and relaxes until Brandon arrives, there's nothing else to do. The house is clean, laundry is done, scented candles are burning on the table and plug-in air fresheners all around the house.

She answers the phone baby I'm here. My GPS says I will be there in 35 minutes. I can't wait to kiss and hold you. I miss you so much Brandon can't wait until you get here. Is there anything you want to do today? Nah not really, we can chill for today, cook something in the house or we can grab something quick from a restaurant. I just want to talk about some things, watch movies, relax and enjoy you. Tomorrow we can do whatever. Okay

it's fine with me I'm not in the mood
to go out anyway.

Baby let me get off the phone police
right beside me, she keeps staring at
me. I'll be there in 10 minutes.

She hears Brandon pull into the
driveway and opens the door with a big
ass smile on her face.

Damn Brandon looks good 6'2 Brown
skin, Hazel eyes, low haircut, goatee,
body is on point, 215 lbs. stepping out
of the truck dressed to the tee, black
sweat pant, white tank top, all black
Jordan's, all black watch and a fitted
hat smelling like Versace Dreamer
cologne. She runs towards Brandon,
jumps on him and kisses him in the
driveway. I'm so excited you're here.
Damn babe me too with a smile on his
face let me get my luggage out the
trunk and we can continue in the
house. Kids not, here right? Hell, no
they over their dad's house. He drops
his suitcase by the dining room table

closes the front door, it was a wrap after that nonstop kissing taking off each other clothes Brandon pick Keisha up walks to the couch laying her on her back kissing on her ear, neck, moving slowly down to her breast every passionate kiss and lick on her body made her pussy even wetter more than he even imagine.

I swear he was eating like he was starving, and I was here to make sure he was never hungry. He slowly puts his dick into this ocean waters it sure felt good the deeper he went the higher the moans got. He looks into her eyes as she puts her nails into his back sucking on his neck. She leans over the arm of the couch as he fucks her doggystyle pulling her hair until they both climaxes.

Damn babe your sex is so good and always on point, I need to take a shower, now baby which way is the bathroom as he picks up his suitcase,

Brandon upstairs on the left side come on I will show you. Thanks baby I didn't realize how big this house is you doing your thing huh. I try; go big or go home as she laughs so I guess size does matter. So, why do some women say size doesn't matter"? It's the motion in the ocean. Because they are always shorthanded lol, I prefer big, thick, and a great performance in bed umm like you Brandon. Someone that has the package and knows how to use it very well.

You funny as shit with a smirk on his face, baby come get in the shower with me you ready for round two. Yup you talk a lot of shit Brandon, I know but I always back it up with no complaints you can vouch for that. Whatever let's see how you hold up in the shower. Water hitting their bodies long passionate kisses he leaning on the shower walls she moves into a squatting position while the water is running through her hair as she is sucking the hell out of his dick then starts to teabag him, he grabbing her hair embracing the sensational feeling on his dick.

She gets up and her back is against the wall with her legs wrapped around him. They both heavy breathing moaning through the roof. He's going to work in her pussy as if we are making a porn video after an hour, we both wash our ass then got out of the shower.

Keisha what's for dinner we can either go out or I can cook, it's up to you. Well since this is your first night I would rather stay in and have you cook. I hope you know how to cook. I'm not trying to get sick from salmonella. You must not know who you are talking to. I'm the best chef you ever met. I throw it down in the kitchen.

Yeah!!! Yeah!!! we will see sex is different from food. You have tons of jokes today but either way you will always stay satisfied. I aim to please with a smirk on his face. So, what do you have a taste for Ke? I don't know whatever you feel like cooking. Okay let's go with chicken, shrimp and broccoli alfredo, is it okay if I go in the kitchen to make sure you have everything if not, we either change plans or grocery store here we come. Go head it's fine. Alright you have everything but the broccoli I can work with that. So, you making this from scratch Babe, hell yeah that's the only and best way, buying the store-bought shit is ok if you're being lazy but if you like your food fresh; cook that shit yourself and it tastes better. Dinner is served so "What do you think?" It looks good but let me take a bite. Oh my god I just burnt my tongue, it tastes okay I guess I'm just playing you did your thing it's good and no I'm not just saying it. You were supposed to blow on your food to cool it down before eating it. I just took it off the stove Ke.

Now we can get to the bottom of conversations we had previously that's important. What you have on your mind Brandon? So, what happens between you and your ex on vacation? Babe I told you nothing happened he tried to kiss me. I pushed him off and told him I love you not him. Why do you keep bringing this up? That shit bothers me what you want me to do, not say shit you got me fucked up. Another thing is the conversation you had with the dude about me because he feels some kind of way when we talking, or you mention my name I'm not understanding if you are no longer with him. Lord Jesus Tim wants me back. I don't want to be with him, and he knows it, this is his way of getting back with me in his head to try to interfere in what we have.

I don't know what you want me to do. I can't control him. How do you think that shit makes me feel? Keisha put yourself in my shoes, that shit doesn't feel good. You right you can't control him, but you can control yourself and stop telling him, our business knowing he wants you back. I understand but what the fuck you want me to do he should know something about you and for real I never said anything bad about you for him to react in any kind of way towards you; that's just who Tim is.

Yeah, alright I'm not here to argue with you I needed an understanding if we together it's only you and I. So, what you needed to tell me since you want answers to your questions huh Brandon. Remember when you first met me, I was bartending and dancing, later that day or the next day I told you one day I wanted to own a construction company.

Yes, so I'm not understanding just say it. Before I met you, I have been owning my construction company for 4 years now it took off more than I thought it would. So why did you lie about that and what's the point to still dance and bartend? I like money but I only dance twice every month and with bartending I do it in my free time or when someone calls out if I'm available. I dated women that wanted my pockets and liked my physique. I reached a point in my life where I wanted more than someone just wanting me for what I can do for them or the fact I look good.

It's more to the man than just physical and financial so I vow to myself next time I meet someone she would only know the basics of me far as my career bartender and male exotic dancer, until I found the right one and it's you baby. Well, I was thinking something way worse than this, I truly understand but

I would never be with a guy just for his money nor his body. Brandon you're in a real relationship with a grown authentic woman who has her shit together in more ways than one, Keisha said. I just knew there was something different about you. I couldn't shake it now I know, Brandon said.

What you want from me as your man? I need you to understand my children and I will forever be a package deal, believe in GOD, unconditional love, honesty, trustworthy, loyal, sense of humor, I need you to protect my heart, you need to mean what you say and say what you mean, follow your dreams, never lose ambition or motivation to become the better you, everything else we can build together. I receive it 100 percent I'm with you no doubt about it.

Keisha, we never discuss children; would you like to have anymore? Because I don't have kids of my own, I

would like two kids. Yeah, sure I would
have one more, but I don't know about
two that's kind of pushing it. I never
explain to you I have lupus, the type
that affects the fetus if I don't take
medication so putting my body through
two more pregnancies is a no unless I'm
pregnant with twins if not only one I'm
willing to have. Baby I'm glad you told
me you sure because we can adopt
when it's time. Yeah, I'm sure one more
child is the max.

Brandon time for Netflix we need to
watch something funny. Maybe a
comedy show you pick Python; for real
chocolate bunny at least, I don't melt;
she spits out her water. I wasn't ready
for that one.

Snuggling up on the couch just enjoying
each other's company was refreshing.
The smell of him, I can feel that he
really loves me beyond his words, the
way he looks at me is undeniable, just
the fact our relationship is peaceful is

always a plus. She looks up at him babe I love you, love you too baby with a kiss to follow.

Three days later we drove to the beach enjoying the weather later that day she showed Brandon the different landmarks in DC. We stopped at the National Harbor Outlet Shopping Center. He wanted to buy some clothes and spoil me which is always great. Brandon brought tickets for the ferries wheel. Lord knows Keisha is scared of heights, but she had to go along with his plans, she had this look of nervousness on her face. Baby you scared I got you; fuck we in this shit together no backing out now, to be honest me being up in the air with little security even though it's closed in don't work for me either but it's something different to do.

Time flew by and we really didn't realize how late it was especially when I'm spending time with someone I love and adore to pieces; time with him is priceless. Driving home babe thanks for showing me a wonderful night, no problem baby. Finally made it home and we took a quick shower before bed. Laying in bed facing each other looking into each other's eyes feeling the love that I thought I would never feel again since my divorce. Brandon, what do you feel about you and I right now? I love you more than you ever know, this may sound odd, but I spoke to GOD and I asked him to give me a sign. If I'm making the correct decision on our relationship, I am not going to lie about the situation between you and your ex-husband kinda had me doubting us. I always follow my heart and ask for guidance along the way. Deep in my soul you will become my wife, my soulmate.

I cannot see it any other way. I'm deeply in love with you. I can't fake it nor hide it. So how do you feel now? I let you completely in, my feelings are everything.

I never thought I would love anyone else, definitely not being in a relationship with someone I deeply love and care about. My heart was guarded, until I met you. When or if we ever get married, I'm not looking forward to getting a divorce I been there done that, and it didn't feel good. My love for you is 100 percent unconditional and comes with no strings attached, I love you to pieces Brandon.

He caresses her face with his hands while gazing into her eyes kissing her forehead as the sexual chemistry intensifies. She climbs on top passionately moaning, kissing and biting his ear, moving to his neck down to his 8 pack, now getting his dick wet with my nice warm saliva as it gets harder and harder.

My pussy is awaiting his 10 inches to satisfy me and damn sure hit my Gspot as I sit on it with a loud aww sound as he enters me. Riding him like I've never done before as his dick slowly goes in and out making me horny then before, he pulls me down as we kiss, and I whisper "give me that dick" make my pussy cum all over your dick. Baby damn I want you while rolling over now he's on top dog walking the shit out my pussy like he's Jordan trying to make 3 pointer hell winning the championship trophy.

Now I'm in this weird position left foot on the bed right foot on the floor, left hand on the nightstand and the right hand on the floor holding my balance, he fucking the shit out of me as my ass bounce up and down on his dick. We both talking nasty moaning louder and louder as we both cum.

Next morning Keisha's in the kitchen cooking breakfast Brandon is upstairs getting himself together. All of a sudden she hear keys in her door.

Good morning Keisha, "What are you doing here Tim"? "Where are the kids and why in the hell you have keys to my house"? The boys forgot something, and I made a copy of the kid's keys. Is it a problem? Yes! It's a problem and I told you if they forgot anything, I would bring it over, why didn't you just buy it from the store like you said, you gotta go Tim right now.

While Brandon comes down the stairs asking Keisha;" Baby what are you trying to get into today?" whatever you want babe. Tim go get whatever you came here for, nah you have playboy in my house. Brandon hears the conversation and comes to the kitchen. My name is not playboy homie, it's Brandon I would have thought you learned that by now. Man, I don't give two shits what your fucking name is why the fuck are you in my house. Hold on, this is not your home anymore you made your decision and besides, you not supposed to be here, did you forget especially without calling, please go get what you came here for.

Keisha fuck what you talking about why is playboy here. Tim, I'm not arguing with you. Why are you asking her ask me don't get mad because you see her moving on to a real man that treats her like the queen she is, you dropped the ball, just move off the court time has ran out and there won't be any resets trust that. Shut your bitch ass up if I want Keisha back, she knows what it is. I guess you didn't tell him about Hawaii huh, she's the mother of my children. I will always be in the picture whether you like it or not.

You funny as shit for real man; what you consider a real man bartending and stripping get the hell out here you barely can support yourself. You miss me with that bullshit. Tim get the fuck out my house you starting shit, and nothing happen between you and I in Hawaii while she standing in between Brandon and Tim. Nah Keisha move the fuck out the way it seems like pretty boy Tim has a lot on his chest he want to say so what is it my nigga stop playing wit me.

Oh, so you didn't tell him how we was kissing and damn near made love, because you know it's a difference between fucking and making love playboy with a smirk follow with a laugh. Keisha holding on to Brandon as he pulling away is this shit true you only told me y'all kiss you left out y'all was making out and damn near fuck what kind of fool you think I am, fuck that get off me Keisha for real. Tim walks off to get whatever the boys left, comes back and says bingo Keisha I told you a man always has insecurities and I just found it. Have a nice day while laughing, walking out the door.

Keisha threw a cup at Tim.

Baby nothing happens between us I stop it before anything could go farther, I'm sorry I love you so much.

Fuck you Keisha take the love shit out of it I'm packing my shit going to a hotel remember this if you don't remember shit else 90 percent of our life, we can change the other 10 percent we can't. If this is how our relationship is going to be, I don't want it, every time I see your ex-husband, I'm not trying to argue with dude c'mon now.

Please don't leave can we talk this out he wants this to happen you leaving so he feels like he has the upper hand. Nah not right now maybe tomorrow but I'm done talking. I 'DON'T WANT HIM' Brandon stop letting him win.

What else do you want me to do? Brandon I'm tired of going back and forth with you about him. I want you to respect me as your man. I might call you later bye Keisha. She screaming, food burning she exhausted of Tim bullshit she takes the pan off the stove throws it in the sink, crying this is not how this is supposed to be after opening up my heart again for love, this could go up in smoke literally. She called Brandon babe can you just come back, Man look I don't feel like talking give me some time bye.

Now she is calling Tim. Why are you trying to destroy my relationship? That shit isn't right, I never did shit to you and Brandon didn't either get your shit together it's over you did that to us not me. Now that I'm happy with someone else that's not you, my life has to be miserable because you're not happy I don't think so.

I'm done with your immature bullshit grow the fuck up Tim. Ladybug I'm happy for you however no man is being in the house that we built from ground up, my money paid for that not his. Tim you on this power ego trip bullshit we agreed the house is mine through our divorce and I put money into the house as well.

Move on to the next best thing like you always have. Bye I can't with you, and I won't we are not together, nor will we ever be back together. Ladybug tell baby boy I said get his emotions together. Yeah whatever, have my kids call me later.

She just doesn't feel like eating anymore. She needs to find a way to get her man back. He doesn't deserve none of this. I'm stressed out. I don't know what to do. I'm not getting Tanya and Angel involved in my personal business. Who can I turn to? I guess I can call my mom but I'm too old for that and besides, she has her only life now I'm back at square one again. Keisha sits in her backyard with the bottle of wine next to her feet listening to music to ease her mind. I'm tired of crying going through the same shit why can't he just see I want him? We just talked about where we wanted to take our relationship now this. He needs to look past Tim fuckery and realize he has a grown ass woman in front of him.

She poured cup after cup to deal with her emotional roller coaster. I promise myself I would never let another man put me in this situation ever again now here I am. Keisha get yourself together. You are not doing this right now as she giving herself a pep talk.

To relax even more she takes a long hot shower after she gets out, she makes a chicken salad with another bottle of wine and cozy up with the couch watching TV. Several hours have passed since talking to Brandon. Keisha speaks with her children for an hour just checking on them. She passed out on the couch and slept until the next morning.

Phone constantly ringing knocking at the door she can't move that fast wiping the coal out her eyes morning breathe isn't pleasant and this damn hangover, she trying to find her slippers hitting her toe on the corner of the coffee table yelling at the door HOLD ON I'M COMING she opens the door WHAT I'm not buy no more cookies.

Babe it's me Brandon what cookies? Baby I'm hungover I drank two bottles of wine and I thought you were some of the neighborhood kids selling cookies again, it seems like they know when I'm going through something.

He laughs, you going to let me in or we going to stand outside. Oh yeah, I'm sorry come in can we talk now baby.

Yeah, I'm in a better place to talk without anger but you sure cause the wine is taking effect. Yeah, Brandon

I'm fine. Let me just start off by saying I apologize for my behavior yesterday, very unacceptable towards you, but what pissed me off was the fact I'm hearing shit from your ex that you left out on purpose I don't appreciate another man telling something about my lady first when you should've told me.

You're absolutely right but nothing happens, why you can't see I'm here for you and want you. Keisha that's why I'm here if it was someone else my ass would've been on a plane going back home. I'm not ready to give up on you and I, when I said I'm all in this is what I meant I'm showing and telling you so there won't be any questions unanswered. Besides I'm here for three more days I couldn't go back home knowing our relationship has a disconnect. I sincerely apologize for putting you in an uncomfortable situation babe, I'm happy your back.

Keisha, I have some things lined up for us to do tonight but before we get to that; let's get into this. He picks me up carries me upstairs right there. I knew it was on and popping. After an unforgettable love making sessions, we begin to get ready for whatever B (Brandon nickname) had planned. She put on her most sexy dress with her most expensive heels to compliment her man, and damn did he look good dressed up.

C'mon baby this is by reservations we can't be late. What do you have up your sleeve? Babe, you will see. We arrive at this nice restaurant/lounge for spoken word in which I never been, but always enjoyed on TV. I love poetry. It brings feelings, emotions, understanding to life. How did you know I would like this? I'm speechless. Baby you forever writing in your blue journal and you forever telling me how much you like the words of art in poetry, so I thought this would be breathtaking.

I pay attention to the small details in my relationship, especially about my partner. She hugs and kisses him. You are truly a good man that's why I love you. This is not all in-store for tonight Ke, really what else could it be she thinking to herself. Will he propose what should I say he hasn't met my children yet and his conversations with Tim never went well, so what else could it be?

Chapter 22

"Finally Moving On"

Ladies and Gentlemen let's give a round of applause to Brandon Smith, wait they calling you why, just sit back and listen. Good evening everyone this is for an incredibly special lady in my life, here we go with soft jazz/blues feel plays while he starts.

Keisha you are the anchor to my boat, the waves in the ocean that speaks. My glorious sunlight is like a bird flying so freely without missing a beat. You are who you say you are, and I couldn't ask for anything more. I'm your Black King and you're my undeniable Black Queen, breathtaking when you enter the room you have my purest heart as he gets on one knee "Will you marry me"? She's crying nodding her head YES, she leans in for a kiss baby I love you, love you too. The crowd is clapping saying congratulations. She staring at him you are so amazing I couldn't ask for a better husband. Brandon you need to meet my children, baby I already did. What, wait when that happen. It's ironic Tim called me yesterday after everything happened and invited me over so we could have a talk man to man. Tim basically said if I'm going to be the man in your life, I needed to meet the kids and I agreed.

We both agreed we were out of pocket but we both understood our place when it comes to you and the kids. I can't believe he called you, how did he get your number. I assume he got it from you, nope not at all the only time he had my phone is when he was taking pictures on vacation, sneaky ass Tim. So, how did the kids react towards you?

The oldest was cool about it, Johnaya and Elliott were asking questions so we could get to know each other and Alim quiet but observing everything. I understand the emotions and questions I'm someone coming into their lives, so it's expected for any push back even anger I get it. Elliott is a firecracker so if he didn't go off the handle, he must like you. Nah he was pretty cool about everything.

So now that everyone is on good terms what is the next step for us Keisha now that we are engaged. Well, your career is in Vegas and mines is down here so we gotta meet in the middle, but for me I can't just uproot my kids like that and especially away from their father. How about this? After we get married for the first year, I will stay with you for 6 months and you and the kids come to Vegas for the other 6 months or after school is over. By then that would give each of us time to get everything in order for our companies. Placing someone in a position to run our companies that we trust. For me I would need to travel back and forth to Vegas twice a month to make sure everything is running smooth besides via Facetime and phone calls. Okay I'm fine with that so what happens after the year B?

I will move to Maryland and start my construction company down here as well; I took in consideration about the children, so I don't mind moving besides I need a different scenery anyway, but I still need to travel back to Vegas to check on my company tho. No problem baby it will work itself out. I'm ready to go home unless you still want to stay. Nah we can leave. You don't know how nervous I was to ask you especially in a room full of people I didn't know, my palms were sweating, hands were shaking hoping you said Yes. I couldn't tell you. No, I was surprised you asked me, I know we talked about it, but I didn't think it would happen so soon.

Before I left Vegas, I already had it in my mind that I was going to propose to you. So, I went to several different jewelry stores until I found the right one and of course I asked the young lady for help and she showed me different rings but this 30 Karat Emerald-Cut Sapphire and Pear-Shaped Blue Diamond Halo ring I kept looking at, so I bought it. Babe, it's an unbelievably beautiful ring but I don't need all this; something simple would've been fine. I'm scared to ask how much it cost? You probably wouldn't want to know Keisha.

Now I want to know how much was it? Uh ummmmm.... Over $50,000 bands. What the fuck I'm taking this ring off and you can get me a cheaper ring, you know what we can do with $50,000 and a ring isn't it. Ke, I'm not taking the ring back so put it back on your finger I meant to buy the ring for the purpose of me marrying you and the price I didn't care about. Babe that's too much for a ring. Keisha put the ring on your finger, nothing is going to change the price or me taking it back. Alright I'm putting it on, I'm so ready to get in my bed and relax. This day has been exciting, overwhelming and beautiful and I must say I'm so cheery.

Me too baby as he lays on the bed with his clothes still on, she kisses him babe you gotta get up take off your clothes so we can go to bed. Alright I'm getting there I'm tired he finally gets up to go to the bathroom to brush his teeth and to take his clothes off. By the time he gets in bed Keisha damn near sleep as he kisses her on the forehead, Goodnight Love.

Good Morning Sleepy head breakfast is served in bed thanks baby you didn't need to fix breakfast Ke, it's funny because I had the same idea for today. I was going to get up before you fix breakfast. I guess I drop the ball huh. Nope not at all I know you were exhausted and besides this is how a relationship/marriage is supposed to work together and not against each other. Keisha turns on the shower to start her day, babe I need to stop by my office and stop by Tim's house if you want to come.

Yeah, I will come let me finish my breakfast and I will get in the shower with you. Well hurry up I need my sexual fix in the shower; shit I'm done now that's all you had to say. He stands behind her kissing on her neck while his hands caress her breast. She turns around kissing nonstop he started to suck and lick on her nipples as if he was looking for milk. Brandon made love to every inch of her body he wanted to finish on the sink counter.

Keisha sits on the sink counter back against the wall as Brandon proceeds to please me as we both climax as she sucks all the cum off his dick.

We both got ourselves together after a wonderful start to our day. Driving to the office babe I'm so elated I can't believe we're engaged. I never thought I would even consider getting engaged or married after Tim and I, but you came along and gave me a different outlook on marriage, I really appreciate that. Ke you not the only one even though I never been married nor never met someone I would even think about asking to marry me, I know for sure that I made the right decision when I asked you. Hell, fifty bands on a ring I knew you were the one because spending that kind of money on anyone I never did, and I wouldn't just do that kind of shit. I love you so much I never felt this way about no one. Love you to Brandon.

Babe, I don't know if you remember Tanya and Angel crazy selves, but they will be at the office. Yeah, I remember they seem cool why what's up with them. Nothing but when they see you tons of questions will come especially from Angel nosy ass, Brandon laughs alright. Keisha and Brandon walk in. Baby sits in the waiting area. I will only be a quick second.

Good afternoon Angel, Hey Boss Lady with a smile on her face "How are you doing Python"? as she looks at Brandon. Hi Angel but it's Brandon not Python. Tanya comes out of her office to say checkmate Angel your ass is just nosy, I know I'm nosy but I'm not crazy his name is Python right at least it was in Vegas. Yeah, Angel his stage name is Python, but Brandon is his government name. Sorry for being rude; Hi Brandon, naw you cool I'm good.

Tanya enters Keisha office; Hey lady, how has everything been? I can't complain, I have my kids and my fiancé's life is good. Wait what fiancé you and Brandon. Yes, he proposed to me two days ago, girl I was shocked even though we had several conversations about marriage, but I didn't think he would ask me this quick. Angel being nosy asking Brandon "Did you propose to Boss lady"? Yes! I did propose to Keisha. Do you think it's too soon you know she went through a lot with Tim and I can't see her go through that again? I understand your concern and the love you have for Keisha but I'm not here to put her through the same thing Tim did nor will I be compared to him and his actions, we are two different men. I love Keisha and her children and if Keisha and I want this relationship to work it will work. When I proposed to her my heart was and still is 100 percent in this relationship and soon to be marriage, I do not play with my feelings nor would I play with someone else I am deeply in love with her.

Okay I hear you and I must say y'all look so cute together, so you have my approval, Angel told Brandon. Keisha, Are you ready for marriage again? Tanya asked. Yeah! It's not like we are getting married tomorrow. We still have a lot of things we need to figure out. Okay just take your time and do not rush into anything. Tanya, I am not. I love him. Brandon and I will figure out anything pertaining to our relationship.

Was there any luck on Tim house searches? Yes, but it does not have everything he is asking for. So, this house entails 6 bedrooms and 5 bathrooms, 8,2035sqft, open floor plan, gourmet kitchen, indoor/outdoor pool, bowling alley, movie theater, and it's not too far from where you live Keisha. But it doesn't come with an indoor basketball court, listing price

$8,000,000. I did find cheaper houses but none of them compares to this one especially because it has the majority of everything he asked for. Thanks a lot Tanya I'm stopping by Tim house later on and I will give him the update more likely he will take it. I will speak with the real estate agent that listed the house after I speak with Tim. Keisha and Tanya walked out the office, Congrats Boss lady on your engagement Brandon and I was out here talking. Oh, okay thanks Angel, how is your pregnancy coming along in a little while maternity leave huh? Yeah, I can't wait to see my bundle of joy because I'm tired of using the bathroom every 2 seconds, my back constantly hurting can't ever get a good night sleep. I understand the feeling. Keep me updated on what your doctor says and when you go into labor. Call me if you need me, see you Monday morning.

Babe: Angel did not give you a hard time, did she? Nah she just wanted to see if I was a solid guy and was here for the right reasons. Okay she can be a little much sometimes. So, we are on our way to Tim's house so I can see the children and discuss some business about the houses. Are you okay with going over there? I know you and Tim had a kumbaya moment.

Yeah, it's no problem we two solid men and we stand by our word family first and respect will always be there as long as lines don't cross. I like to hear the two men in my life are getting along because one thing is right, family comes first Tim is the father of my children and you're my fiancé and I couldn't deal with the bickering. You right but I would not call it bickering were men we call it letting our present be known, whatever B it's all the same.

She knocks on Tim's door, Hey Ladybug, nothing much needs to discuss the houses and see the kids. Well okay! Khalif is at his summer art program and Alim, Elliott, and Johnaya are somewhere around here. What's up Brandon I see you ask Keisha, nice ring choice. Yeah, it went better than I thought, so what you been up too, nothing much hopefully Keisha found me a new spot to move in too because my lease is almost up and for real, I'm not trying to sign another lease with them. I feel that all the money you spend on renting someone else's apartment or house hell you could've brought your own. Exactly Keishaaaaaaa come on so we can talk what's the update on the houses. Okay I had my assistant help me find some houses for you we found several however it was one that stuck out the most. 15 minutes away from the neighborhood in which I live. Six bedrooms and five bathrooms, 8,203sqft, open floor plan, gourmet kitchen, indoor/outdoor pool, bowling alley, movie theater. Here are some pictures of it if you're interested; we can schedule to see it in person.

Okay, Ladybug my basketball court is missing, seriously Tim with all that space you can build an outside court besides once you hear the price you may reconsider a basketball court. How much? $8,000,000. Tim and Brandon damn near spit out their drink. Are you fucking serious 8 million dollars of my money Keisha what happen to 2-3 million dollars? Look Tim I was trying to give you everything you were asking for unfortunately this is how much it cost but everything is negotiable in real estate.

They are asking for prices in our kid's college funds and bank accounts apiece, but I trust your judgement and I want to make an offer for 7.1 Million. You sure Tim? Yeah, I'm sure it's closer to my family hell yeah make the offer and see what they say. Give me a sec she steps away to call the realtor. Hi Jake, Hey Keisha I have an offer for your property listed for 8 million dollars. Okay Keisha is this a good offer, Yeah, it's a great offer and if your client is eager to sell, they would take 7.1 million that is the highest my client is willing to go. The offer is way below our asking cost and my clients may not budge on the 8 million dollars. Okay how many offers do you have at the moment the house has been sitting on the market for over 6 months and I know for a fact your clients never came close to my offer because if they did, we wouldn't be having this conversation right now, so call your clients and call me back. Alright Keisha I will call you back.

Ladybug, what did they say? Jake is calling his client to see if they accept the offer. Worst case scenario is they can counter or deny your offer completely. Hold on Tim, Jake calling back.

Hey Jake, did they accept the offer, nope they counter for 7.5 million are you serious do they know this is the best offer they would ever receive. What must I say they drive a hard bargain, give me a sec Jake so I can talk to my client?

So, Tim they counter for 7.5 million it's up to you I would say 7,350,000 all-cash offers closing in 10 days. Yeah, go head these motherfuckers smoking they bet not counter shit else I couldn't do this for a career I would've lost my mind. Alright Jake we're coming back at 7.250 million all cash offer and closing in 10 days. Okay we accept congratulations to you and your client Keisha same to you Jake nice doing business with you. Everything will be typed up first thing tomorrow morning talk to you then, okay.

So they accepted 7.250 million I

thought you were going with 7.350 million, when your opponent hears you say cash offer most of the time, they will accept the offer especially when they don't have any other offers. Congrats Tim you deserved. Time to celebrate! Brandon, you want a drink. Yeah! What you have? Anything you can think of dark/ white liquor, some beers in here. Let me get some Hennessy. Ladybug you want something. Yeah, water is fine. So, how long are you down here for? Man, I leave tomorrow I need to get some shit in order for my construction company I have out there. Okay!! That's what's up. So, you no longer dance or bartend? You trying to be funny, Tim. Nah I'm serious so how is everything going to work out when y'all tie the knot.

I plan to stay in Vegas for 6 months and the other 6 months Keisha and the kids can stay with me in Vegas if that's fine with you.

Hell, nah that's not going to work I love my kids I can't be away from them for 6 months. Did y'all both bump your heads? Let me make this easier for everyone. Our kids can go to Vegas for 1 month during summer break, the other part of the summer they stay with me.

I'm with whatever you and Keisha agree on, our plan wasn't to live in Vegas. Keisha already told me that couldn't happen so after we get everything in order I'm moving down here.

Come on now Tim you know I wouldn't never take you kids from you I'm fine with one month in Vegas. More likely I can't stay the whole six months myself because the kids' schooling and Angel going on maternity leave pretty soon, so there's a lot of things I need to sort out like Brandon, and I spoke on. Okay as long as you and I have open lines of communication for our children and always put mature thought into what's better for them. I'm fine with everything else. No problem Tim I agree. Well, we gotta go. I will call you later on.

Well, that went good with Tim normally he's an ass, but he changed for the better. You know him better than I do but I understood where he was coming from and couldn't do anything but respect that. Absolutely baby what you trying to get into this is your last day before you leave. I want to get into you as he laughs but for real let's grab some crabs. Maryland is known for their blue crabs right. Yes, we are and what you know about it. Nothing much! Tryna see what the hype is all about because a crab is a crab. Yeah, whatever you need to try it with some melted butter and mayo/ketchup mixed together, child you don't know what you're missing. That shit sounds nasty as fuck babe I will pass on the homemade sauce, crabs only with seasoning. Your loss not mine. How do you like the crabs so far? For real I don't see any difference from any other crab I ate.

Keisha I really enjoyed my week with you and meeting the children, a lot has happened, and I appreciate every situation good or bad. You and I being engaged will always outweigh the bad, that was and is a special moment love you.

Aww babe love you too thanks for being patient and understanding to my needs, I can't wait to be called Mrs. Smith. Babe tomorrow I need to be at the airport by 8:00am so we need to get it in so I can get some kind of sleep. He wakes her "Get up baby I'm leaving I will call you when I get home" as he kisses her before leaving.

Chapter 23

"Stressed Out"

She walks into work thinking about the proposal and how stressful planning a wedding could and can be trying and wanting to make sure everything is perfect. So much on her mind all at once. Now that she is in the office, back to work mode. Keisha checks on all the real estate agents working in her office to make sure they all is up on their work and satisfying each and every one of our clients, constantly hosting open houses to bring in potential buyers, other brokers.

As she makes her rounds to everyone office, she receives a call "Hey Keisha within the next 2 weeks I'm moving into my house so I will need for the

children to stay over for 2 days until everything is completely moved in",
Also I hired a contractor to make the plumbing, electric outlet, etc. is up to code. That's fine. Why are you saying it like they don't live with me? Nah I wasn't saying it like that I have them for summer break that's why, calm down, you sound stressed don't take it out on me.

Sorry I can admit when I'm wrong and yes, I'm stressed to a certain point about this wedding, but I'm not going to sit here talking to you about it. Why not? I'm the best candidate to talk to hell. We were married for several years. Because I'm not it's inappropriate I'm at work I will call you when I get off or shoot you a text. Several weeks later Tim has informed me that he will need to stay with me for about a month or so until electricity and the installation is brought up to code, I just can't with all this stress.

Hey love, how is your day going? Well, it's pretty stressful planning a wedding in a different country not knowing if everything will go as planned, work has been hectic with clients, paperwork. Oh, Tim has to move back in for about a month as she mumbles it under her breath. Hold up!!!!! What you just say? I'm stressing about the wedding. Nah after that, work has been crazy, stop playing you know what I'm talking about you said something about Tim. Oh yeah, I did, didn't I. He has to move in for about a month until the contractor fixes his electricity and something else and brings it up to code. Why can't he stay in his apartment or go to a hotel until they finish. His lease is up, and he refuses to sign for another year and for the hotel, maybe he's trying to save money, I guess. So where is he sleeping? In one of the other rooms definitely not with me if that's what you're asking. Just to let you

know I'm coming back down in a
couple of days I tied up some loose
strings so we will see how this works
out your ex-husband and me all in the
same house. Well, it has to work for the
kids' sake I'm not putting up with no
drama from either of you.

C'mon now you know the bullshit never
comes from me, you right but it seems
like Tim is in a better space besides, he
can stay in the mancave. I never
change it. So, what do this mean for
you and I when it comes to sex having
a full house. What you mean this house
is way too big we can find some places
and besides, we do have a bedroom
that comes with a lock door just saying.
Damn you're a smart ass let's see if you
have all that mouth when I get there.
You already know what my mouth can
do and being smart is just one of them.
Yeah alright, I hear you back that shit
up when I have your ass bent over
fucking the shit out of you. Oh, ummm

whatever as she laughs.

Babe I know you said you were able to tie up some loose strings, but did you put anyone in charge for the time you're not down there. Yeah, I did. My brother is in charge. He knows the business inside and out he was there from the beginning. Oh, okay I still haven't had time to find someone to take over for me. I was thinking about Tanya, but I guess we will see.

I'm so stressed babe about this wedding you want over 200 people and I understand but that could become costly. Then you want to fly out some of your family members. I understand maybe your parents, grandparents and siblings but everyone else needs to find their own way there.

It's too much already talking to someone overseas and wondering if they understand our vision for the wedding because we can't be there 24-7 to visit and make sure shit is in order so, the stress of flying this and that person out is overwhelming. To be honest babe I prefer to have a small intimate wedding with less than 75 people. How about only inviting 125 people which would alleviate some of the stress, I definitely don't need you stress; hell, that's going to cause problems between you and I which I'm avoiding at all cost. Brandon that would help a lot however we need to think about your parents, grandparents, my mom and children on a flight more than 7 hours to Paris, "Should we change the location"? Nah we are not changing our location everyone would be fine and besides it our day not theirs, if they come, they come if they don't, I'm fine with that too. Stop overthinking shit everything will work itself out.

I just want everything to be perfect because this will be the last time, I'm walking down the aisle, so do you have

any groomsmen in mind and the color
you'll be wearing? All my brothers and
we are all wearing blue so we can look
like blueberry pimps as he started to
laugh, no the hell y'all not, baby I'm
joking I just wanted to lighten up your
mood but for real I haven't given the
colors any thought. We can discuss that
when I come home in a couple of days
if that's fine with you.

It still sounds weird when I say home
meaning your place, but I can get used
to it been as though you are my soon
to be wife. I can get used to calling you
my husband and sharing my space
because you know sharing is caring.
WOW! Did you hit me with the
preschool shit sharing is caring?
Laughing her ass off I sure did.
You have a lot of jokes tonight, I'm
bored; Why can't you come tomorrow?
Let me look over some things I
probably can come 2 days early, but I
want to make sure I don't put my

brother in a bad spot especially if he has things to do before I leave. Okay understandable babe I'm going to sleep I need to get up early I will call you tomorrow after work. Love you, love you more.

Chapter 24

"Handling Business"

Good morning Tanya, I wanted to talk to you about something serious so if you have a minute, we can discuss it now before everyone arrives. Okay no problem is everything okay? Yeah, everything is fine, I wanted you to take over for a couple of months while I take some time off, so you will be the overseer for everyone that works for the company, etc.....

For real Keisha I would be delighted to take over but let me move some things around first. Okay just let me know when you are officially able to take over in the meantime, I will finish with all my clients.

Okay I'm so excited I'm glad you see

the potential in me to put me in charge; no problem you already doing everything. You know the business inside and out, so why not. You're right I have been in the field for about 4 years now I'm confident to take on the role in which you are giving me you won't be disappointed. Girl, do you smell that? What? My coffee girlllll it smells good and definitely tastes good. Do you want some? Yeah, I will take a cup or two, don't be drinking all my coffee now as they laugh.

After a long day at work Keisha relaxes in her hot bubble bath with rose petals with a glass of wine lord knows because in a couple of days, she will have a full house with Brandon and Tim in the same space for a long period of time. I will definitely need a therapist after this.

This could be a good trial run on how the children interact with Brandon and how Tim is receptive of the situation. In the meantime, I will enjoy my peace, sanity and a noiseless home. She just remembered to call Angel back after she called out of work today due to her doctor's appointment.

Hey girly, "What's going on any updates"? Yes! So, boss lady I'm a high-risk pregnancy so my doctor wants me on bed rest asap. So, I will finish the rest of this week and half of next week until you find a new receptionist. Okay! Your health and the wellbeing of the baby is more important to me so take all the time you need. Just keep me informed about the situation even after you have the baby.

Also do you know anyone with a receptionist background in real estate. Yes! I do he just received his real estate license so I think he would be a great fit. Keith and I were just talking about him finding employment. So, this is good timing for him.

Okay tell Keith to come by the office

sometime this week and the job is his. For real boss lady I can train him before I go on my doctor's orders. Okay! Angel stop calling me boss lady. I understand why you do it, but Ms. Keisha will work. Okay! Boss lady see you tomorrow. Bye Angel.

Chapter 25

"Late Night Conversations"

Tim, why are you calling me so late? What's wrong? Are the kids okay? Yes! They sleep; soooo "Why are you calling"? I need to stay longer than what I anticipated. Why? What happen to a month? I'm having other things done. I need it to my liking. Seriously you acting like you're not trying to move in after spending millions of dollars. No! I'm moving in 100 percent and the kids and I are coming earlier than what I told you so Friday after the kids summer programs. Whatever don't bring none of your shit, but 2 bags don't need you getting comfortable. He laughs alright gotcha bye.

She calls her mom; girl you know I'm sleeping. "What the hell you want"? You know Brandon partially moved in. Tim needs to move in more than a month, children will be home, and you know how Tim is. I thought he just bought a house I'm not understanding why he needs to move in.

Have you told either one that they will be sharing the same space? Yeah, I told B and he's fine with it as long as boundaries aren't crossed. Tim having work done to the house personally to me the house is perfect but of course he is who he is. Good luck this already sounds stressful. I can come over for a couple of hours.

Just let me know what day this is about to feel so awkward. How you have your fiancé living with your ex-husband, Lord Jesus you have your work cut out for you. Mom, you're not making this any better, but I get to see how we all get along as a family.

You know Tim speaks his mind he doesn't care who is around and Brandon is the same way, 2 alphas under the same roof. Girl call me in the morning. This is too much for my brain cells, goodnight ma.

Before Keisha goes to bed she checks on the kids and calls Brandon afterwards. Hey Ma, I met Mr. Brandon when dad invited him over. Why didn't you tell us about him? Elliott because your father and I were going through a lot in our marriage and to be honest I didn't want to

bring another man around you
or your siblings before the time
was right.

You know I'm not calling him
dad, daddy, in any form because
I have a father. How long have
you been dating him? Little over
a year and half. So, how do you
like him? Ma he's cool for right
now, but I will be watching I'm
very protective over you.

Also, dad introduced us to his
outside child claiming he's our
brother, so I asked dad where did
he come from because ma only
has 4 kids, and he isn't one. Then
he explained everything that he
did and the reason why y'all no
longer together.

I was upset for a while towards
him. Baby there's no reason to be
upset towards your father things
happen and situations change
either for the best or worst

unfortunately, our was the worst, but your father and I co-parenting very well and in a better space. Okay ma I gotta go, my friends back online time for Fortnite. Okay love you see you tomorrow. Love you too.

He needs to answer this facetime; What's up baby? I can't believe Tim told the kids the reason why we got a divorce we agreed that we were going to keep it between us. Calm down he did right as a man he probably wanted to relieve the hurt he caused and was carrying.

I'm pretty sure every time he looks at the children, he knows he's the reason why everyone is no longer living together, and his family is broken up. Ke just leave it alone don't jump down his throat he has the right intent. I'm sorry babe I didn't ask how

your day was, it was chill for the most part making sure everything was in order before I leave tonight and see my sexy fianceé and have family time. Oh, okay ummm so you ready for this adventure everyone is outspoken in their own way babe, ummm this will actually be your second time around my family and not just for a week. Yes! I'm ready for whatever comes my way. I stay ready so I don't need to get ready, stop overthinking. I'm trying it's just nerve wrecking knowing I have my fiancé and ex-husband in the same house. I get it Ke but if there's no feelings between you two then; What's the problem? You act like he's staying permanently.
It's just temporarily right we can act like we have some sense especially in front of the kids.

Yeah, I guess it won't be so bad everyone I love is under one roof, a girl couldn't ask for anything more.

So how much do you love me is it enough for me to blow your back out, I don't think my fiancé would appreciate you talking to me like that. Your fiancé is a lucky man. I wish it was me and not him for real. I wonder if he realizes how great of a woman you are or better yet how a person like you is one in a million. I wonder too, so babe do you realize what I have to offer and what I bring to the table? I love the role reversal we gotta do that more often yes, I realize it; why do you think I just said what I said.

Now you being a smartass what time you coming tomorrow because you know I get off work at 4. Yeah, I'm being a smart ass because you know how I feel about you and to answer your other question not until 6 or so, all the earlier flights were sold out.

Do you need me to pick you up at the airport? No, I didn't want to wait for a later flight so I'm driving from Vegas to you. Besides, I'm staying for a while there's no reason to rent a car for several months when I can drive my own car.

Brandon, you know that's about a 36 hour drive you sure you want to do that. Yeah, I'm driving right now as we speak after a certain number of hours I'm stopping and getting a hotel room. Sleep a couple of hours and back at it again. Baby be safe and don't overdo it speeding and shit. I'm good baby I will be fine, get some sleep. I will see you tomorrow evening, and I will text when I get to the nearest hotel in about an hour. Love you big head oh, really okay love you too.

Chapter 26

"Safe Travels"

Next morning, she woke up too missed text message, phone calls, and voicemail. As she's cooking breakfast she listens to the voicemail: Good Morning sunshine you still must be asleep. I just left the hotel this morning and I'm back on the road, call me when you can, see you soon baby love you. Smiling ear to ear what a beautiful start to my day while eating her breakfast and having a cup of coffee. She calls back; good morning B you put a smile on my face every time I hear your voice, so you listen to the voicemail huh, yeah fool why you think I'm calling you back. Maybe because I thought you miss and love me, I do, and you have jokes early in the morning. Did you sleep well last night? Not really, I hate staying in hotels unless I'm on vacation besides, I didn't have you laying next to me to ease my mind.

I should always be on your mind whether I'm there or not, stop playing with me you know damn well what I meant. I thought I had the jokes but you trying to be funny. You can't be the only comedian in the relationship, well Ke keep your day job, jokes just isn't your thing leave it to the pros. Fuck you Brandon how about that as she laughs yeah alright, we see if you have that smart mouth when I see you keep that same energy, you already know I aim to please on all levels, mentally, emotionally, spiritually, physically and sexually my job is to know your body inside and out literally. I like when you talk to me like that it makes me moist, baby, where are you?

I'm about 8 hours out, Why? Where are you? In my truck driving to work. I want to play with my pussy. I'm horny. C'mon you gotta wait for me baby it's only 8 hours don't be selfish remember sharing is caring.

I said I wanted to, how can I do that and drive? I'm not crashing my truck. When you horny as hell you will find a way don't act like you never have. Boy bye I'm at work now, I'm all man been past the boy stage see you around 7 or earlier.

Chapter 27

"New Receptionist"

Grand rising ladies, nice to see you Angel how you feel? I'm pretty good but this morning sickness is kicking my ass. Ms. Keisha, Keith will be here shortly. Keisha turns around with a smile okay Angel. Tanya walks into Keisha office and closes the door behind her.

Can we talk; yeah of course you have this glow about you Tanya what is it. It's not really business related, remember the guy Johnathan? The name sounds familiar but not really. Why am I supposed to remember him? No! But yeah, he was our limo driver in Vegas, okay just spill the beans. Jonathan and I are officially a couple, hold on I damn near choked on my coffee say what; I'm confused you barely talk to him so how we get here. When he drove us to the club, he whispered in my ear can we exchange numbers I didn't do it right there. Where was Angel and I? Drunk out y'all minds. Yeah, I was drinking from the start, middle, and end of the trip I was fucked up huh damn we should plan another trip. Keisha snap out of it and listen so when he dropped us off back at the hotel, I wrote my number on a piece of paper and handed it to him when we got out of the limo.

So why are you just now saying something because I didn't think it would turn into what we have now. You aren't right Tanya holding secrets from your girls' shame on you. Angel, how can you hear our conversation? The door is closed duh. Tanya through the intercom on the phone it does connect to the boss lady office and by the way Keith is here.

Angel you nosy as hell can't nothing get pass you, supersonic ears and shit. Well, congrats to you and Johnathan I'm happy for you both there's nothing like being loved by the right person. Angel sends Keith in please and no eavesdropping. Hi Keith, Angel has informed me that you're looking to work in the real estate field and how you just received your license.

Yes! Ma'am I switched career fields. I was tired of retail in the sense of working for someone else and making peanuts when they receive the full course meal off my hard work. I want to be my own boss with guidance from someone of your caliber.

I understand this is a temporary position until Angel is able to return to her full duties but if you allow me to prove myself, I would love to be a part of your team.

Well let me enlighten you; real estate is

not easy sometimes it's a hit or miss, after saying that let me say this if your motivated and dedicated you will reap the benefits, everything doesn't happen overnight and if you think that's how it happens because you watch real estate TV shows and see the glorious side that's not it. There is a lot of disappointment and questioning is this the best career move, but if you stay with it, I can honestly say benefits are bigger than the reward. When can you start? I can start today. Oh, okay I will see you Monday 8 o'clock sharp. Thank you so much I won't disappoint you. I know. Well ladies goodnight see you Monday oh Angel Keith starts Monday at 8.

Chapter 28

"Full House"

As she drives, she receives a call; Hello Ladybug, the kids and I will be there in 20 minutes are you home. No not yet just leaving work just let yourself in the kids still have their keys right. Yeah, I just asked them. Were you cooking or did you mind if I cook? Uhhhhh I really didn't plan on cooking, but you can if you want too. Tim let me call you back Brandon calling, alright I will see you at the house. Hey Babe, how far are you? GPS said I will be there in an hour, but I need to stop for gas. Will you be there when I get there or are you still at work? I'm driving home now, and Tim and the children will be there.

No problem I can't wait to kiss and hold you it's been a while.

Who are you telling I want you more, more than you ever know, Ke tonight I will find out how bad you want me and oh yeah, I didn't forget about your smart-ass mouth from last time?

Oh, really you know you can't handle my mouth or anything else, what I tell you about being a comedian telling jokes just isn't your thing, you know how I get down. But on a serious note, I didn't know what the kids like so I will rather give them money if that's fine with you, yeah, they would like that, but you don't need to do that. I know I don't need to do it; I want to do it. Tim is not going to feel any kind of way, is he? He shouldn't but whatever.

True but I'm not trying to step on that man's toes, babe it's not that deep it's for the kids if he catches an attitude, he will get over it because the kids aren't going to give back the money. I finally made it home and I will see you when you get here babe, alright I'll be there in 20 minutes. Keisha walks into her house no one is to be found. She hears noises walking towards her son's bedroom, opens the door and he's yelling at his friends on Fortnite, come here and give me a hug.

I miss you, come on ma you messing with my game; boy please. Where is your sister and brothers? Also, where is your dad? Seriously, ma they somewhere around here. She sees her daughter talking on the phone. Hey ma I'm getting the Tea give me a second ok miss you too, yeah ma I miss you too. What in the world going on around here Keisha checks on her other two sons both sleep but where is Tim. She checks the mancave he's not there just when she turned around, he was standing behind her: you looking for me? Yes! It was quiet in here until I heard Elliott but "Where did you come from"? I was sitting in the backyard just thinking as they stared into each other's eyes.

Okay! What were you thinking about? For real Keisha like you don't know, I really don't know Tim what it is. Nothing at all. I'm about to take a shower I will be upstairs in 20 minutes to finish cooking. What's wrong Ladybug I don't think your man would like you downstairs with your ex-husband while I'm taking a shower we can talk after I get dressed.

She holds onto the door and yeah, you're right see you upstairs. She hears Tim yell "WHAT THE FUCK" as she walks away knowing this will be a long and hard several months revisiting her old pain that she thought was over and done. She laid on the sofa relaxing with her glass of wine trying not to engage in what just happened, so she turned the TV on and listened to her daughter spill the tea.

Shortly after that Tim comes from the mancave with a look on his face baby girl can you let your brothers know dinner will be done in 45 minutes. Yes! Daddy besides, I need to get the full tea mom I will talk to later with the other cup period pooh. Keisha laughs she is something else she acts just like you, naw that's all you to the fullest attitude and all.

Damn he smells and looks good and that smile is everything. "So, you are really going to go through getting married again"? yeah why not B is who I want to be with. No reason just asking I couldn't get married again I'm one and done, you say that now until you find the one for you. No, I'm pretty sure. Yeah! Yeah! whatever you say. So how is work going? Fairly good, very busy but I plan to take some time off to handle some personal business. How about you? I can't complain business is

steady. What else can I ask for.
Baby, "Can you go get the kids for
dinner"? I'm sorry let me rephrase
Keisha can you please go get the kids.
Uhhhh yup I sure can but you know
you can't call me baby. Can you get the
door? No problem he walks over to
open the door; What's up Brandon,
nothing much man "Is Keisha here"?
Yeah, she's probably upstairs. Alright let
me take my luggage upstairs and we
can chop it up when I come back down.
Tim, "Who was that"? "Why didn't you
tell me he was coming"? Because I felt
like I didn't need to. Why in the hell
you feel like you didn't need to tell me
we were all going to be under the same
roof. Uh because it's my house and we
are no longer together. So, you're going
to play me like that okay I see you, Tim
not right now. Yeah, okay dude
upstairs looking for you. She gives Tim
the side eye as she walks away.
Keisha enters her bedroom where

Brandon is hanging his clothes up in the closet. Brandon gives her a kiss. I was waiting for this moment as he picked her up and she wrapped her legs around him, I really missed you baby; you look good. Thanks babe and you looking like a full course meal and a snack as she laughs, really with a smirk on his face.

Baby I'm about to take a shower and freshen up that drive wasn't a joke do you want to join me? I do babe but Tim cooking dinner and it should almost be done, and the kids are waiting for us to come downstairs.

I understand give me 30 minutes, you got it babe as she kisses him and leaves the room. We were all sitting around the table laughing and joking when Brandon came down to join us. Babe you want me to fix your plate. Nah enjoy yourself I got it.

He finally sits down good evening everyone, Hi Mr. Brandon, just when it seems to get awkward there's a knock on the door. Keisha answers the door while Tim says you have a lot of surprises tonight huh, Brandon looks at Tim with a smirk. I'm never a surprise. Hi Ma and Niecy pooh I'm glad you'll be able to join us because I need more estrogen around the table and less testosterone. How is everyone holding up, especially my son's in law? Look at my grandbabies, pretty and handsome as they can be.

Y'all hungry, no not really, we just ate something before we came over. Both said at the same time ma to answer your question, you can't be serious right now Brandon wait your turn I was here first; business is okay taking one step at a time just trying to become a better me.

You done; like we in kindergarten or something taking turns, Ma I'm looking to open my company soon down here, and planning the wedding, spending quality time with Keisha and the children and being happy.

Great, I hope you both work out whatever it is because this tension is thicker than a snicker up in here. Tim, ma is right can we handle this like men and talk in the backyard if you up for it.

Yeah, let me grab a drink Keisha you have some Hennessey or something strong around here? Downstairs in the mancave by the bar nothing changed Tim. Alright Brandon grab the cups because you need a drink too.

While the men are talking Keisha needs time to talk to her mom, if y'all done eating you can remove yourself from the table while I talk to grandma. I just don't understand the push back from Tim he created this situation and now that I moved on, he wants something different but it's a little too late.

Well baby unfortunately that's how men are they want their cake, ice cream and a couple of meals on the side, then when they see you moved on to something better than them all of a sudden, he wanna come back. Yeah, but my door is closed I cannot allow myself to go backwards when I have a great man in front of me, I'm not saying Tim isn't great but he's just not for me anymore, but I don't think he understands that or maybe he just doesn't care.

No! He understands but he also understands how he fucked up; Brandon is a good guy and I see the way he looks at you there's an undeniable bond that you both have follow your heart because your brain is already there.

Yeah, I know I wonder what they out there talking about she walks over to the patio door and slightly opens it. She hears Brandon say man what's up with you it seems like it's a problem because I'm here; I thought we settled any problems we had prior so explain bruh. Look here man I don't explain myself to anyone let's set the record straight hell yeah, I felt uneasy with you here.

You talking about staying under the same roof with my children and wife then I'm still paying all her bills. Why wouldn't you think I will have a problem? Nah she's your ex-wife is what you meant and "Why are you still paying her bills"? That's what real men do but now that you're in the picture all bills due by the 5th. I have no problem taking care of home trust that, do you think this is easy for me because it's not, but we need to find a common ground for the next couple of months. Also, Tim you may not like me, but you will respect me all the slick remarks end tonight. I like how you are trying to put your foot down, but that shit doesn't work like that, not with me anyway.

Yeah, alright we can agree to disagree the same way you want respect show me respect and we will be all good. Brandon, look man I'm going through a lot right now, I'm done talking about this bullshit, but I hear you. Respect remember that shit goes both ways. She hurried up back to the couch acting like she wasn't eavesdropping while finishing the conversation with her mom.

Sooooo... "How did everything go"? Hopefully, you guys were able to come to a mutual agreement and level of respect. Keisha, can we talk in private? Yeah, What's wrong? Why didn't you tell me Tim was still paying your bills? Seriously right now Brandon he's still paying my bills because it was a part of our divorce agreement, I didn't need to tell you about it because it wasn't your business and at the time, I didn't know you.

So, you still gonna let him pay all the bills, are we really doing this over some fucking bills Brandon. I'm not trying to argue with you get your shit together it's not like I'm fucking him. It's a fucking bill a piece of paper. What the hell you mean it's not like y'all fucking? Do you want to fuck him is that why you said that Keisha? You gonna stop playing with me for real, if I wanted to fuck him I could have as she walks to the bedroom door, Brandon blocks the door, so she won't leave.

Did you lose your fucking mind talking to me like that, nope not at all but you can move, you're the only one having issues with him paying my bills, now if it's such a problem I will send all my bills to your email monthly. We will finish this conversation later, yeah whatever are you coming back down to join everyone else. Yeah, I'm coming give me a second. Please get your shit together before you come back around the children. Keisha you pushing it. She walks out and slams the door behind her.

Ladybug is everything okay? Yeah, everything is fine, never been better. Tim can you go get the kids for family night. Just when Tim walked off ma you were right, having two alphas in the same house may not work. It's stressful already on day one. Child, I don't know what to tell you I think deep down you knew this would happen this is what you choose now you gotta ride it out. Yeah, but I thought we were in a better place especially between them after their talk.

Where is everyone, we might need to start this movie, yeah Tim is taking forever, and Brandon still didn't come downstairs. Ma can you check on the children and please don't get lost. I will see where the alphas are as she laughs. She checks her bedroom, mancave, backyard, swimming pool and neither one is there. She hears talking; Brandon and Tim playing basketball; she didn't want to interrupt about time they were getting along.

Ma, I guess it will be just us watching a movie if you're still up to it. No, it's getting late and you need time to sort things out with your family so we are about to go, I will call you tomorrow. Okay since you're leaving, I'm going to bed and hopefully everyone is on a better note, love y'all. Baby, you sleep. I was before you woke me, "Why what's wrong"? I want to finish the conversation from earlier. Look I'm not getting in between you and Tim ego trip both of you need to get your shit together and I understand how hard it is for you and him being in the house knowing that Tim is my ex-husband and you're my fiancé.

I would probably feel the same way if the shoe was on the other foot, but there is a level of respect I have for both of you and also our relationship is on different levels. Well Damn you didn't let me get a word in I was only trying to apologize for earlier I let him get under my skin.

I had to release some tension, so I played basketball the reason why I didn't come downstairs, which gave me a better outlook on things I just needed time to myself. Little bit after I guess Tim was looking for the kids and we ended up playing 21 and we had a heart to heart without the bullshit, the love and respect we have for you.

We agreed nothing is more important than you and the kids and our difference as men doesn't matter. I'm glad you both had another conversation because I didn't want to be stress or have the children see you and Tim going at it over some dumb shit. Both of you mean well so we are going to leave it at that.

I'm going back to sleep now, so I can't get any. Nope! you fucked that up earlier and I was going to wear my fuchsia lingerie with my handcuffs, and you could have had your way with me. Seriously you can't reconsider. Turn off the lights nite nite love you, yeah you don't love me that much as he mumbles under his breath, what you say? I said nothing, goodnight.

Next Day, the smell of breakfast in the air. She wonders who's cooking? Only to get to the kitchen with no one in sight, but a plate on the kitchen counter wrapped up as she assumed it was her breakfast.

Where is everyone? They have a problem disappearing as she is talking to herself, this damn house is way too big to keep walking around here. She calls Brandon "Where are you?" babe we all downstairs at the pool, okay I'm coming now.

Good Morning, y'all thanks for making

breakfast my ass was exhausted from last night. Y'all don't think it's too early to go swimming; nah the kids enjoying themselves and Brandon and I chopping it up talking about our companies, never know we might go into business with each other.

Oh really, so how is this going to work? Tim you own a landscaping business and Brandon own a construction company am I missing something.

Babe, yeah you missed it we are not merging our companies together but starting an upscale men's suit company.

Sounds great and both of you like to dress up and you both look good in a suit, so why not.

For real Ke, yeah for real Ladybug that's how you playing us, as they both looked at her and laughed, Keisha pick up your face; we just playing. HAHA what made y'all even talk about starting a business together, after getting to know each other we realize we both are solid dudes, we have the time, money, and we are like minded when running a company so why sit here and constantly arguing with each other when we can muscle all that energy in getting the bag.

Besides what man doesn't like to look and smell good especially for their woman on date night, damn Brandon you know I'm single I still like to smell and look good though maybe I will find someone to take on a date.

Ummmmmm what happened to Brittany? Did you ever get the DNA test? Nope! She refuses. I still see him, but only on her terms. Why are you letting her control when you see your son?

Too speak honestly because a part of me feels like he's not my son, but I don't wanna feel like an ass if he is. I haven't done shit that's why I deal with her and them dumb ass terms. Look Tim I know I'm just the mother of your children and I don't want to overstep my boundaries, but you need to take her to court and keep a record of everything you buy, phone calls and text messages so you can have proof. Damn, no man should go through all the bullshit she putting you through, I just don't understand women on that level; if a man trying to be there for the kid(s) the mother always give him a hard time, but if you were a piece of shit, she chasing you down making sure you wear the "King Crown" too a man who doesn't deserve it.

Yeah, who are you telling I never thought I would be going through this shit man I take care of all my kids despite how our relationship ended but this right here is on a new level of bullshit.

Well, you always had a thing for thots just saying. I deserve that I'm glad you didn't put me through the same shit. Why would I do that? At the end of the day the only people suffering would have been our children and I'm better than that as a person and especially as a woman. Brandon don't fuck up like I didn't she a good one. Yeah, I know another woman can't even get close to me to where I can smell her breath or perfume because I know what I have at home. We just empty the rest of the "Henny" let me go get some more, babe bring water too.

Children having an awesome time swimming they see us getting along which is great. Keisha, Brandon is a good dude despite our differences don't let what I did hinder you. I see how he looks at you I remember that same feeling but unfortunately, I was too dumb to realize it, until it was too late. I really appreciate it and I needed to hear that from you, and I can't lie I had so much anger towards you but I'm glad we're in a better place friend. So, we upgraded to a different level in our relationship huh Ladybug, I like the sound of that friends. Tim joined the children in the pool just when Brandon came back out. Everything is looking up for the better babe, yeah, I know this is how you wanted it to be. Everyone being honest and respectable to one another is always the key to our healthy relationship. Aye y'all not getting in the pool? Yeah, I'm kind of tipsy, No I'm going back in the house and enjoying my peace and quiet. Who's cooking dinner tonight? Let's flip a coin, Keisha it looks like you cooking tonight. How did I get thrown into this, it was supposed to be between you and Brandon, we just decide now it's your turn? I bet y'all did. Is it the chef choice or did you 2 have something in mind? It's your choice.

Well, I'm going back in the house. I have some writing to do. Baby I will check on you in a little bit, okay babe. She lays on her bed and reaches for her poem book on the nightstand. How is your writing? It's going.... Just wrote a poem called:

"My skin color is Beautiful" for everything going on in this world. We need a change. I have 3 upstanding Black Kings and 2 Beautiful Black Queens I'm raising. Keisha you only have 1 daughter, yeah, I know Brandon but I'm including my niece. It was just something on my heart and besides, I just like poetry you know that. Yeah, I do let me hear some of it if you're willing to share.

"My skin color is Beautiful"

What is the difference between our skin because when you tear away my beautifully made dark brown skin, I am a different color which matches yours and if we cut deeper enough, we bleed

the same color the children of GOD so who are you to judge me or better yet make the judgement that I'm a threat, aggressive, bad, or unpredictable in a way to make yourself secure in your own insecurities? I'm not here for you to read the certain pages of my book in which sooth you, but for you to understand you are not my GOD no judgement of me that crossing your lips will be cast upon me in which your lies will not be buried in to my soul nor will I speak in a manner that has no purpose you will not hang me with cuts, bruises, and unwanted touches, on your truth GOD has sacrificed his blood, pain I stand on my own 2 feet to tell you FUCK YOU and I'm here I'm not going nowhere.

It's deep I love how your words have meaning I can feel and understand the passion and pain within the poem, keep it up Ke. Thanks, I appreciate it. Well now I wrote a little and took care of some other paperwork. I can take care of you. Oh, really let me lock the door as she lay on the bed signaling for him to come over. He climbs on top of her kissing non-stop until she tells him to stand up on the bed with his back against the wall as she politely unbuttons his pants and proceed to give him the best head he ever had. All he can say is shit baby I was missing this, while grabbing my hair, just when it felt like he was going to explode in my mouth riding his dick felt more pleasing.

Just as my pussy sliding up and down the tip of his dick was harder than ever; he told me to get up and start fucking me as if I didn't something to him; Damn, babe what I do to you? As he whispers in my ear your mouth remember. Just when I was about to climax, he hands me a pillow bite this your too loud as my overly wet pussy explodes on his dick and just when I thought it couldn't get any wetter or messier the warmth of his cum graces my face.

Damn, baby I needed that quickie. I told you to make sure you still had all that mouth, I thought you forgot because you didn't mention it. Nah I was waiting for the right time to get your smart ass back, whatever shower time then I gotta start dinner. Keisha tomorrow Tim and I taking the boys to a basketball game. Okay look at y'all getting along and shit well I guess me, and little mama can get our nails done and go shopping.

After the dinner Tim receives a call and excuse his self suddenly you hear him say; are you fucking serious right now where the fuck is Brittany, alright I will be there in 45 minutes to get my son. Ladybug you won't believe this shit Brittany left our son at her cousin house now her cousin calling me because Brittany texted her saying she was staying over some dude house and for her to call me to come get my son. So how long do you think your son staying at my house, Keisha for real right now I already have so much bullshit. Yeah, that you created don't get mad at me "So how long"? Ke not right now you see he gotta get his son. Brandon stay out of this and I see that he needs to get HIS son. The key word is HIS; Just to remind you both……. but you know what; he can ONLY stay for 1 week and everywhere you go he will be right with you. So, when you go to work don't forget him.

Alright Keisha let me just go get him. Brandon so you think it's right for me to be reminded in my own house of the infidelity that Tim was doing and as a result of it he has a baby by Brittany. Fuck no! But what I'm saying is the baby is innocent and caught up in Tim bullshit and right now you see this man going through, so why come at him like that. You don't think I don't know the baby is innocent however I don't need to see a constant reminder.

You men are all the same, you do shit then think the woman is supposed to deal with your bullshit and since you think so Brandon here is your cover and pillow, sleep your ass on the couch, Goodnight.

Nah hold up I'm sleeping on the couch because I don't agree with you right now. You wrong I'm not saying you're wrong for how you feel, but what Tim did to you, you shouldn't take it out on the baby. And just to clear it the fuck up all men is not the same don't put me in the same category as Tim or any other man because I'm not them. Since you're on some bullshit I will be glad to sleep on the couch and hopefully in the morning you have a new motherfucking attitude.

Several weeks later Keisha is loving the

way Keith is fitting into her real estate company and Angel is on medical leave due to her doctor's orders and Tanya finally takes her place until she gets everything in order at her house.

Hey Tim, can we talk it's been several weeks, and your son is still here. So, what's the deal with that? Keisha look; I know you are not fond of my son being here, but he is my son, and I will not put your feelings over top of what I need to do for him. Right now, his mother is not being a mother to our son and rather run the streets and my son will not be a part of her dumb shit. Let me stop you right there Tim I'm not saying put my feelings over top of your son but what I'm asking is consider the hurt you cause among the family you had before this one, that's not too much to ask.

Did you really ask your children how they felt when you brought him around? It's just not about you Tim maybe for a change consider the children you had before him and maybe you will understand where I'm coming from. No, the only conversation I had with them was letting them know what happened between you and I, and the aftermath of my action I had a baby outside of our marriage then I introduced him to them. That's my point.

Brandon walks down to the mancave Tim you ready to go. You still not dress. Yeah, I was trying but Keisha needed to talk so here we are, "Where the hell y'all going"? We going to the bar. Soooo "Who is watching"? Never mind I will watch little man until y'all get back besides "What is his name Tim?" Timothy. Thanks ladybug I really appreciate it no problem that's what friends are for right.

Ke, can we speak upstairs? What now? I wanted to say I love you and appreciate how you put your feelings aside. Therefore, you're my fiancée soon to be wife. Come here give me a kiss damn you smell good so y'all just going to the bar. What else up y'all sleeve? Maybe a strip club or two with a smirk on his face I'm just kidding. Yeah whatever, have a good time. As they both walk downstairs Tim has Timothy in the highchair feeding him, thanks ladybug for watching him. Brandon now is you ready let's go, hell yeah. Just when she didn't want to get close to Timothy, she grew to care for him as if he was her own. How can I resist that cute smile and his cute little face just in a matter of two hours? She had a talk with her children to accept Timothy with open arms even if he's not biological my son, but he is your father's son which makes him your brother. Something is just meant to be the way they are. It seems like they all had this nonchalant attitude as they agreed to try which reminded me, they are so much like their father in different ways.

She finds a cartoon movie to watch while the older children off doing their own thing. As Timothy and I lay on the couch watching the movie we both ended up falling asleep until Brandon and Tim walked in. Why are y'all so loud do you realize it's like 3 something in the morning.

Brandon why is there a scar on your face? and Tim what the fuck is wrong with your hands? I'm confused so one of you needs to enlighten me right now. Tim you wanna go first, hell naw she your fiancée you go first, really, she was your wife before she was my fiancée. Seriously y'all talking about me as if I'm not standing here so what happen.

Alright Keisha so we went to the bar/lounge in DC everything was going good Brandon and I talking and drinking. We were talking about my issues and some other men's things. Some dude approaches me thinking I was talking about him for some reason and he starts talking reckless out his mouth and you know I don't like disrespect. As much as I was telling homie I wasn't talking to him he was still coming at me, but I guess it was because his friends were hyping him up.

Dude swung at me and I beat the shit out of him and he still picking up his body off the floor. I broke the chair across his head long story short his friends hyped him up to receive this ass whooping. So that doesn't explain what happened to your face, his friend tried to jump in it. He caught me 1 good time and that was all he wrote because I punished the shit out of him so now, they both helping each other off the floor.

That bar is fucked up as they both laugh man I haven't been in this kind of shit in a long time. But that's not even the end of it we left and guess who I see Brittany with her new dude. When she saw me instantly start talking shit so now, I'm going back and forth with her. She really got mad when I told her dude she's like the 7-11, customers come and go. Of course, he got into his feelings. I politely let him know I don't mind handing out ass whooping.

I can't with neither one of you look good when you leave and come back all jacked up. How was little man? He ate all his snacks, played with Alim, then him and I watched a cartoon movie until y'all two fools came in here with all this noise. Oh, I did have a conversation with our kids about accepting Timothy with open arms, they gave me this nonchalant answer hell they get that from you. Make sure you get the bag of broccoli to put on your face just to make sure no swollen starts and for you the bandages in the medicine cabinet wrap your damn hands up.

I'm going to sleep can't believe y'all out there acting a fool, as she walks away. Yells get "Timothy off my couch".

Next morning Keisha lays on Brandon's chest while he plays with her hair, Keisha I know it's been a long couple of weeks for you and myself, but we need to get back on track with planning our wedding. Yeah, I know but I just been so drained from work and everything going on at home I kinda lost focus. What made you bring this up? The last time we talked about the wedding was before I came down here. Baby can you get your notes so we can go over everything, I still want a wedding in Paris at least 100-125 people.

Babe, didn't we have this conversation already about lowering the people. Yeah, we did but I also lowered the numbers at first it was 200 people, I think. I really want a winter wonderland wedding but very intimate,

"What do that consist of"? A winter wonderland theme wedding everything is white with beautiful blue lighting, snowflakes, ice icicles, etc..... So far, I like your theme but let me google a winter wonderland wedding first because you realize we're not getting married in the winter right. Duh! Brandon, but we can bring winter to our wedding with the right venue and wedding planner. You right! okay I see what you talking about it's kind of girly for my taste, but I can picture you walking down the aisle in your beautiful white gown looking stunning, so I can look pass the girly touches.

So, I guess my tuxedo will be a light gray/silver color. So, colors for the groomsmen/best man and maid of honor/bridesmaids? I really didn't think that far, me either. So, did we ever talk about budget baby? Well, if we did, I don't remember but since we are on the topic, "What is the budget

Brandon"?

There's no limit it's whatever you want but I know how you are; so, what about $400,000 this should cover everything if not there's still no limit.

Did you lose your freaking mind I was thinking maybe $75,000-$100,000 if this doesn't cover everything, we're going to the courthouse? Just because we have the money, we will not spend tons of it on a wedding to only last a couple of hours and especially for everyone else. Alright Keisha you got it. I understand as long as I make you my wife, I'm down with whatever. We can finish speaking on this later the kids and I made plans for me to take them shopping. "You coming Keisha"? Maybe when? In 15 minutes. Seriously, that doesn't give me any time to get myself together. Come on you can throw on a hoodie you already have pajama pants on, besides who is going to be looking at you. Everybody is going to look when they see my swag in my pajama pants hell my next fiancé/husband might be at the mall.

HAHA yeah you sure about that I will lay hands upon him, sike nah if he looks, I know I have a gorgeous fiancée, that's all he better do is look. You're a piece of work come on make sure you have your wallet and keys because I'm not driving nor am, I paying.

I already knew that you not saying anything new, whatever let's go.

Several hours later finally made it back to the house, kids bouncing off the roof Brandon damn near brought the whole damn mall, the kids just picking up shit just because.

Everyone needs to meet in the living room in 10 minutes for our family meeting.

Ok the reason for this meeting; Hold on." Where is Timothy?" He's a part of this family. He's playing with his toys. No! he needs to be a part of this.

Ground rules: I have all this testosterone in this house. I need my grass cut, pool clean, dishes clean, toys picked up, house clean spotless daily, do I need to go farther. Timothy can pick up behind himself who cares if he's 2 1/2. This is a team effort just saying y'all driving me crazy around here. Yeah, we all hear you captain I guess after we finish doing mom's list of chores "Dad, do you want to play ball?" Yeah, I need to release some stress. Mr. Brandon you can join us 2 vs 2, alright no problem Tim you cool with that? C'mon man yeah, I'm cool with whooping your ass, yeah, we will see who has the last laugh whoever scores 60 points first wins. I hear everyone talking but no cleaning is getting done. Damn she has supersonic ears for real.

Yeah, I heard that too Brandon. Man get used to it; there will be times when you're thinking about something she would answer as if she can read your mind, you're absolutely right Tim as she walking down the stairs. I thought maybe we all would be on the same page in reading minds I guess not because the grass isn't cut, and the pool isn't clean... At least I walk pass the kid's room.

I see their room is decent and even Timothy is picking his toys up, so I'm confused with y'all. Baby I'm not in the mood to clean the pool right now, so when will you be in the mood? Tomorrow morning, I got you. So, since you want to clean the pool tomorrow you don't mind cleaning the bathrooms all 5 of them.

Naw, I will take a rain-check on the bathrooms and I would rather pass go and collect $200 and clean the pool, that's what I thought. So, Brandon you thought you were getting off that easily, you have a lot to learn my brother I damn near choked on my water listening to you trying to get out of it.

You better learn to say, "Happy Wife Happy Life", or it's going to be "Angry Wife Unstable Life". I guess you would know about the "Angry Wife Unstable Life". So, you taking low jabs now; yeah, alright let me cut this grass before it be "ex-husband beating fiancé ass".

You funny as shit Tim keep cutting the grass that's what got your ass in trouble the first time; with them damn quotes, is that what you said to yourself "the grass is greener on the other side", until you figure out otherwise. Man am I supposed to be in my feelings right now. Nope! You can't be in your feelings about facts just saying.

Chapter 29

"Keisha's Staff'

Hey Tanya, how is everything going at the office? Hey Keisha, everything is going fine for the most part, but that Keith is something else. He is forever flirting with our male clients. I spoke to him about it but he's exceptionally good at his job. I can say that.

For everyone else they are staying on top of all their work and we are closing sales left and right. Okay good to hear. I'm glad you spoke to him about it because the last thing we need is for our clients to feel uncomfortable and we lose their business.

How have you been holding up besides the office? I can't really complain. Jonathan and I discuss taking our relationship to a new level, so everything is going great with me. How about you? Girl it's been crazy Brandon and I wedding plans down to Tim moving in for a couple of months until he finishes some work to his house, kids outta school for the summer and now Tim son lives with us. I just have a lot on my plate, but I can at least say I love having my family around me. Brandon and Tim are getting along which is always a plus.

Let me call you back Angel calling on the other line. Hi Boss lady, seriously Angel what I tell you about calling me boss lady, okay Keisha. Anyway, why didn't you tell me when you get in the 3rd trimester you sprinkle a little pee, weird cravings, your feet swell, and it throws of your PH balance girl I never had a yeast infection before now I'm just itching glad my doctor gave me some medicine because lord knows I thought my fiancé gave me an STD it was about to be war.

 Angel that was an ear full for real um everyone pregnancy is different, and I didn't want to scare you. Every woman's body changes in different ways especially after having the baby so be prepared for that. How have you been feeling? Well, I love the fact my fiancé caters to me, but I hate being in bed all day. I like to be out and about. I understand that completely. Keisha let me get off the phone. He thinks I'm resting, girl bye.

Chapter 30

"Heart to Heart"

She goes to the kitchen and notices Johnaya and Timothy watching a movie. Where is your father? Oh! He took Khalif to his art program so Brandon took Elliott to basketball camp because dad told Brandon he had to stop by work, and he wouldn't be back in time. Oh, okay well "Do you want some ice cream"? No! We're fine. Okay! I will just finish doing laundry and working on the wedding plans, yell if you need me. Several hours later Brandon and the boys came back. Ke have you spoken to Tim? No! Not since earlier today, "Why"? Nothing he just seemed off today. He has a lot going on knowing him it has something to do with a female.

Enough talking about him let's get a quickie in. Just when we finally start to get in it good, there's a knock on the door. Hey Ladybug when you're able to come out I need to talk to you. Alright, give me 20 minutes. Damn for real you letting him know how long we fucking. Who cares you need to continue fucking me cause right now you killing the mood? You have a smart mouth let's see if you can take all this dick, long deep strokes while locking his hands into mines. Loud soft moans as our bodies became passionately entwined. The love language of our bodies speaking to each other made our quickie as intense as if we were making love. As we both reached the mountain top to our beautiful feeling of pleasure, I told him don't pull out. Just after we finish, he asks "Do you realize what you asked me to do"? Yes! I know exactly what I told you. Ok! Just making sure it wasn't just the heat of the moment and you really didn't mean it. Let me freshen up to see what Tim wants.

She finally made it downstairs to have a conversation "Tim, what we need to talk about"? Something I've been going through, "Like what"? For starters I stopped pass my house and talked to the contractor so within another six weeks I should be able to move in.

But onto the serious shit my lawyer called me today about the court case for sole custody of Timothy, he informed me that a DNA test would need to be submitted to make sure he's biological mine and I'm nervous as hell. My court date is set for next week. Hopefully, she shows up.

I just don't have the energy to deal with her bullshit. I'm trying to stay on the right path and do the right things. If this little boy isn't mine, that shit would really crush me I love and live for all my kids. So, what if Timothy isn't your son?

To be honest if he's not I can't turn my back on him especially after raising him as my son for two years, then to leave him with his mother whose priorities isn't him nor in order that wouldn't sit well with me. True I understand well I think you have your answer he will always be your son so what you are stressing for.

Because I know if he's not Brittany going to take him from me, she's just a selfish person like that it's all about what's good for her and what she wants. Besides that, I've been talking to someone for a minute now.

You need to slow your ass down with these women and then you wonder why you are in certain situations because you always rush shit, get to know you first. You're right but she's different and she reminds me of you. See you starting off wrong already stop comparing her to me because it's only one me the rest is replicas.

True, but I can see myself with her. I met her on a dating site. We FaceTime each other constantly talking and texting on a regular basis. She's coming to visit in three weeks; she lives in California. So, the both of you staying at a hotel because she's not coming here. Yes of course but I did want to have a couple's dinner at the house I want you to meet her. I'm fine with that. I can see if my mom can watch the children for that night. Let's continue this conversation in the backyard with some drinks because my mind is blown with your stupidity with these women. I couldn't believe you would even fathom a relationship right now with everything going on. As she sips on her wine I'm confused on "why" the rush to be with someone. Keisha, I felt the same way when I found out you were messing with Brandon, but life goes on right. "What you want from me huh," Keisha? I want you not to rush into something just because you feel that you need to be with someone. I want you to deal with shit in a way that you're not bringing someone else in your bullshit. Hell, "Do you really know who Tim is? Real talk I knew who I was when we were together, now I'm just trying to re-learn me again.

My playboy days are over. I'm ready to settle down. You may not like this, but I think I love her. She damn near fell out the chair what you mean you love her. You only communicate through facetime, text messages, you can't get to know anyone just by that. Says who the person that did the same thing now engages with the dude upstairs just saying. Don't do that first of all I didn't plan on nor was I looking for a relationship after our horrible divorce okay.

Truth be told I pushed Brandon away for an awfully long time because I wasn't ready, I still need time to heal from your dumb ass. A part of me was still comparing him to you which put more pressure on me to not give him an honest chance without my baggage thinking he would do the same thing. What's going on here? We're just talking about Tim dating this young lady and how he thinks he's in love. Oh, for real Tim where you meet her? On some dating site I wasn't really looking for anything serious until Stacy and I started to get to know each other a little better. Well, I'm proud of you bruh whatever makes you happy go for it. Alright ladybug can I take you on a date? Stop playing with me Tim everybody wants to be a comedian. Hell, you said it "whatever makes me happy go for it" as he laughs sike nah I'm just joking.

So now you know what's going on with me; "How is the planning coming along with the wedding"? Well, it's going.

It's just frustrating planning, a wedding in a different country because you really don't know if they understand your vision because I can't visit every day to make sure everything goes accordingly. Then on top of it all Brandon wants to invite everyone he knows which is fine, but I really don't want a large wedding. So, what country? And why wouldn't you want a large wedding? This is about him to ladybug.

We having it in France the reason why is because I already had a large wedding and for real do, we really know if the money we're spending on this lavish wedding is even worth the marriage. What I mean by that is; if we spend over a 1 million for our wedding but our marriage only lasted 2 years that shit doesn't make sense to me. I understand what you saying but this man is different than me ladybug u can't keep comparing him to me remember, shit I did does mean he's like that.

Hold on, so you putting negative shit on our marriage and we ain't even married yet that's fucked up. So, what you trying to do because if this shit ain't forever what the fuck are we doing. I'm not getting married to get a divorce no disrespect to you Tim but I'm not a cheater.

I put nothing but work into this relationship. You never had any female call or text you about shit but yet I still feel like I'm paying for some shit he did to you. "Do you really want to marry me or this some get back shit towards Tim"? Look I'm marrying you because I love you to pieces and I know there's certain things I should have been over, but I cannot help to think the maybes. You know what I understand but sometimes love just isn't enough and right now I can feel myself getting pissed so I will be back later. Hopefully by the time I get back you should've

came up with some kind of solution of
how to get out of your own head and
way for a real man to love you
unconditionally, as he slams the door.
Keisha you fucking up I agree with
Brandon you need to get your shit
together and stop living in the past.
I know I dropped the ball in our
marriage but what you were looking
for from me is in Brandon trust that
he would lead and allow him to do so. I
acknowledge my faults in the trusting
department aren't great and I
absolutely need to change my ways
because I'm deeply in love with him
beyond what I can explain.
So now that you know that; be a great
woman to him like you were with me
he deserves it. Let me call Brandon to
see if he answers. I will be right back.
She calls him and notices his phone is
on the nightstand, so she walks back
downstairs. Were you able to talk to
him? No, he left his phone on the

nightstand. Oh, he's really pissed anytime a man leaves his phone and doesn't come back and get it.

Look I made a reservation for a nice relaxing romantic dinner just for you 2. You both need alone time with each other, the kids and I will be fine and to be honest with everyone being in the house and we all have different personalities could be stressful.

Ladybug I made the reservation for 10pm you can go relax for a couple of hours. When Brandon comes in, I will talk to him. After 2 hours he walks in the door "Where is Keisha?" Upstairs but let me talk to you for a second.

Man, what's up now? Man calm the hell down Keisha really in love with you and I understand that you feel like your back is up against the wall because of me and how I treated her but give her some time.

Well let me ask you how long should I pay for your fuck ups, huh? Because I know she's a great woman that's why I asked her to marry me and I'm deeply in love with her as well. You shouldn't pay for my mistakes at all, but sometimes that's how shit plays out unfortunately. Before you go upstairs, I made reservations for you and Keisha to have alone time at 10pm, I sent you the address by text. Okay cool thanks let me smooth this over with her. Baby look I'm not mad at you, let's enjoy this evening and put this behind us. Come here as he puts his hands on her face kissing her "Baby you is all I need" as he kisses her again "I'm in love with you" he slowly starts kissing on her neck laying her on the bed gently undressing her. Babe wait it almost time for us to leave; yeah, I know but we have time as he caresses her body.

Licking and kissing on her inner thigh while his hands are on her breast. She is biting on her pillow so no one can hear the loud moans, as Brandon tongue starts to play with her clitoris, she has her left hand on his head and the other hand gripping the sheets. Just when she was about to climax Brandon gets up and tells her it's time to go, for real right when I was about to cum.

Yup now you know how it feels when you give something your all and come up short. Get dressed so we won't miss our reservation. You just got on my nerves you could have let me finish, yeah, I could've but I didn't. I'm about to take a shower alone, so we can't finish in the shower together Brandon. Not at all I'm good let's just get ourselves together for this nice evening "Can we do that please?" Since you feel like that, I will just take a shower in the other bathroom.

As she proceeded to the bathroom blasting her music putting herself in a calm and relaxing moment to really enjoy this evening Tim has put together for us. An hour has passed, and she is just getting out of the tub filled with a calmer inner peace.

Chapter 31

"Upscale Dinner"

She hears Tim loud ass laughing while Brandon is talking to him. Keisha meets Brandon in the living room as she looks breathtaking with her flirtatious walk towards him.

Damn baby you're very stunning; thanks babe you look good as well. I know both of you are feeling yourself with your conceited ass but my friend who owns the restaurant is waiting for you guys to arrive; and everything you order is already paid for by me. Tim walks them to the door "make sure you bring me back some chicken alfredo". On the way there Brandon turns on some R&B soul music to set the tone. Well, I see you're in a good mood, why you say that because I'm singing along with the song. Yeah, Brandon I never really heard you sing you not too bad either. Love songs will bring that part out of me, nowadays music really isn't the same, the essence of love is lost. He reaches for her hand. This is what love is about trials and tribulations and loving a person not for who you want them to be, but for who they actually are.

As a man I was taught not to get overly emotional or even show my emotions. I struggled with that for years, but I had to come to the point in my life the more I held things in the more explosive I can be. That's why when we get into our arguments, I speak my mind, but I need to walk away to gather my thoughts.

Last thing I want to do is say the wrong thing out of anger and hurting your feelings. Brandon you are my soulmate, my king and my heart. I love you to pieces; Keisha I didn't want you to respond but just hear me out. I love you too.

We have arrived at a very upscale restaurant. Baby tonight is about us so with this being on Tim's dime let's drink up and order everything on the menu as they both laughed. Our hostess walked us over to our private secluded area where the owner met us. He explained to us that Tim called and wanted this night to be perfect for us and anything we wanted he will provide, nice to meet you both and your server will be here shortly.

Tim really went all out huh. Yeah, I guess so. Give me your hands as he reaches across the table; I just wanted to say you are my beginning, middle, end and with that we will encounter our ups and downs and indifferences but with love we can get through anything. Tears start to fall from her eyes as he looks at her.

He starts to cry as he gets up to wipe

her eyes. Baby, "Why are you crying"?
For once in my life, I can actually say I
have a man for me that deeply cares
unconditionally. He leans in for a kiss
I'm forever yours. The server finally
comes over. What can I get you lovely
people? Can u bring a glass of
champagne and surf n turf for me and
can I get something strong with a bone
in ribeye. Okay let me put your orders
in and I will be back shortly with your
drinks.

We really needed this date night to
focus on us. Who are you telling this has
been a stressful but pleasant couple of
months so much has happened? I
wanted to let you know I took care of
the cost of the wedding. I was in
contact with the coordinator giving her
all the information about our winter
wonderland theme wedding.

Only thing you need to do is get your
bridal party, family guest list and
seating together. Oh really, you did all

this "When did you have the time?"
Don't worry about that. No, I'm
worried. How did you explain the
winter wonderland theme? I googled
several different pictures of the theme
and sent them to her.

I spoke to her shortly after that and
she completely understood our vision,
so with that everything is taken care
of. Thanks babe I really hope she
understands because our wedding is
around the corner. Just to make you
feel comfortable we can go two weeks
to make sure everything is in order and
before our guests arrive. Okay I would
love that but what about the children.
They can come with us or come when
Tim comes. It's up to you. Yeah, I
prefer them to be with us. I can't go
two weeks without seeing my kids.
Okay we can look at some places to
stay when we get home. I will need to
return the favor for Tim for putting
this together for us, maybe when we

meet his girlfriend. Brandon, are you ready to go home? Yeah, the food/drinks were great, service was outstanding oh before we leave did you order his chicken alfredo.

I'm glad you reminded me. May we place an order for chicken alfredo yes you may but is this for Tim? Yes, it is. Why? Because he just called and said you were going to forget so he placed the order already which will be out in 10 minutes. As they all laugh this damn Tim, I just can't with him. On our way home just loving the place we are in baby I love you with a smile on his face. We just pulled into the driveway laughing our ass off as we entered the house.

Oh, the two love birds must've had a great time now "Where is my alfredo"? Because I'm hungry as hell waiting on y'all. Tim, where are the kids? They all sleep. Well, my bed is calling for me goodnight.

Chapter 32

"Dress Shopping"

Several weeks later everything was going great, the ladies and I finally were able to go dress shopping. Keisha, "Is that Angel walking in?", Tanya asked. Girl it look like her, but she was supposed to be on bed rest. Hopefully, she stayed home. Couple of minutes past "Hey boss lady" "Hey Tanya" I couldn't miss you in your dress. What kind of friend would I be? Girl take your ass home and you would be a safe and well rested friend at your house. You can have the baby any day now what are you doing and where is your fiancé. I told him I needed to get out of the house, so I was going to my mom's house for a couple of hours.

You are so wrong for lying to him. Look Tanya I was losing my mind every day I got up. I'm greeting the 4 walls because they became my friends. This is how bad I was losing my mind, and besides, he was up my ass I couldn't do shit every little move, he asked if I'm okay.

Which I understood but damn I couldn't fart good without him running up the stairs. Keisha come out so we can see your first dress. Oh, hell no you look like Rose from Titanic next. Tanya you pick that dress out. No! Why would you think I picked it out?

Because it's close to your style just saying. Anyway, the young lady brought the dress out the one that works here for your information Angel. Here I come ladies. I really like this one, Keisha said. Let us be the judge of that. This one is okay but it's missing something. Tanya, I know what these dresses are missing. It's not a screaming bride nor wedding.

Keisha you need a dress that's going to sing to you. In other words, you can't keep your eyes off the same way you can't keep your eyes or mind of Brandon that's what kind of dress you need to be looking for right Tanya. Exactly what Angel just said Keisha. Yeah, I hear you, but I really wasn't trying to spend more than $3,500 on a dress hell even that is way too high. Well, if that's what you spending, they definitely should have better picks. Okay Keisha, try this one on this very beautiful breathtaking ballroom gown. Ladies I think I'm in love with this dress as she walks out Angel started to cry this is the one boss lady can we complete it with a veil. Now Keisha's crying. I can't wait for my baby to see me in this dress.

Girl I gotta go just finish talking to my mom Antonio called looking for me so of course my mom covered for me so I will talk to you later, boss lady you look amazing and Brandon is lucky to have you.

Thanks, girly talk to you later. Alright Tanya everything is taken care of let's go get something to eat. We arrived at some restaurant around the corner from the bridal shop. Girl give me the latest on you and Jonathan. I thought he was a limo driver but he's actually an undercover FBI agent. Uhhhh okay so why was he undercover as a limo driver it kinda doesn't make sense. Yeah, I know I was asking him questions but unfortunately, he wouldn't answer them because confidentiality and his cover may be blown. Well, that sounds like an interesting career to have. Our plan for our relationship is working out better than I thought. So how long will he be in Vegas? I really don't know I'm assuming until his case is over.

Okay Tanya do you trust that he's

telling you the truth? Yeah, I trust him as much as you trust Brandon, what kind of question is that. Well damn I wasn't saying it in a disrespectful way; Brandon and I trust doesn't have anything to do with why I was concerned about you. You know what Tanya I gotta go because whatever is going on with you is bigger than me.

Chapter 33

"Brandon's Secretive

Behavior"

She made it home Brandon you not going to believe the day I had. Why what happened baby I thought you went dress shopping with your friends. That's the problem. I did all that and in return Tanya and I had a talk about the guy Jonathan she met while we were in Vegas. Okay! Baby what's the problem? The problem is I asked her if she trusts him because he informed her that he was in Vegas undercover on a case.

She had the nerve to say I trust him as much as you trust Brandon, like who the hell she thought she was talking too. So, did she say what kind of case he was investigating? No, why? No reason. Where did she meet him in Vegas? He was our limo driver matter of fact he brought us to the club you were working at that night. Oh, really what you say his name was? Jonathan. Why do you need to know his name? Maybe I can check him out to make sure he's an upstanding guy like myself. Baby let's change the subject. Did you like the wedding dress you picked out? Yeah, I can't wait until you see it. What y'all two love birds talking about? Tim asked. Nothing much Ke just letting me know how dress shopping went. Text message comes through Brandon phone baby I will be right back. Time went by Tim talking my ear off about his newfound girlfriend unbeknownst to Tim I really don't want to hear this shit.

After 1 hour she gets up to see where Brandon went, she goes upstairs. She hears the shower water running and him talking "shut it down shit getting hot". Baby, Are you okay in the bathroom? Yeah, babe I'm getting out the shower now. You sure what's too hot? The water. I turned more hot water on than cold, that's all. "Shut that shit down like I said, you know what to do, later".

He walks out the bathroom with his towel wrapped around his waist looking good. He sits by Keisha on the bed in the next week or two. I need to fly out to Vegas to tie up some loose ends, my business partner needs help. Is everything okay with your company? Yeah, but they letting certain people run over them, just gotta make my presence known, I will be back in two days.

Oh, baby I forgot to tell you all my brothers flying in tomorrow to look for our suits they staying for a couple of days. When they fly back to Vegas, I'm leaving as well. Okay no problem. So where are they staying? In a hotel. Hell, no they weren't staying here with us. He kisses her on the forehead looking at her with them bedroom eyes, baby let's get it in. I really don't feel like it. I have shit to do with the kids. I'm tired; baby maybe later. What are you doing with the kids? Just taking them out to spend time with them. Okay cool I will see you when you get back.

Chapter 34

"Trust"

Tim yelled for "Keisha are you ready?"
Yeah, I'm ready Tim where you think
you're going it's only me and kids. Not
at all this is a family outing I'm going
to. Ummmm yeah whatever; you
driving. Hours later we made it back
home and everyone is tired. Brandon
upstairs sleep.
Every part of me wanted to go through
his phone to see who he was talking to
earlier, but I just couldn't bring myself
to do so after all this working on my
trust I had to take him on his word.
After taking a quick shower she lays in
bed next to him just looking at her
amazing fiancé, hoping that he's not
holding secrets. She kissed him on the
cheek snuggle under the covers and off

to sleep she went.

Next morning laying in bed facing each other he gazed into her eyes like something was on his mind. Is everything okay? Yeah, everything is fine I just can't wait to make you officially my wife; And I can't wait to make you officially my husband. Keisha you are everything I imagine and more it was meant for us to meet like we did. I can't imagine my life without you in it, you bring me so much peace in my crowded fucked up world and I love you for that.

Baby I love you too we all have fucked up moments in our lives that we still deal with daily I'm not here to judge you but I'm here to motivate you in becoming the better you. Brandon where is all this coming from? Nowhere it was just on my mind. His phone rings.......... Baby my brothers just landed so I'm meeting them at their hotel. Do you want to come? No! That's your time to spend with them.

We can all go out later on or tomorrow if you want. Alright let me talk to them and see what's on the agenda. Something just isn't sitting right with me on the secretive phone call as if I'm not smart enough to know he wasn't talking about water. Whatever he's doing will eventually show itself. Not to have her mind racing she puts on her two-piece bikini and took a long swim. Hey ladybug, where is everyone? Kids is over at their friend's house and Brandon is with his brothers. Damn you look good ladybug. Can you put some clothes on? It's not right for me to be looking at another man's fiancée in this way. This is my house and my pool hell no I'm not putting on clothes I'm swimming.

Your room is in the basement better yet at your house and speaking about your house when are you moving. Then another thing why are you looking at me anyway when you have a girl. Oh, I see today you're on fire I just came home and you're coming for the juggler. To answer your question, I haven't talked to the contractor since last time I told you, just because I have a girl doesn't mean I'm not still attracted to you so don't get that fucked up, besides that I do have eyes just saying.

Since you're on the edge let me make you a drink because your champagne, you're drinking isn't strong enough. Hell did you eat something? No! not yet. You want some chicken nachos? Yeah, I don't mind. What's going on with you? I just don't want to talk about it. Okay you just been moody lately so I'm starting to get concerned. There's no need to be concerned about me. Tim I'm okay. Yeah, that's what your mouth says but your outbursts and your smartass mouth say otherwise.

Can you just go get the nachos. Yeah, I

guess I can. Tim, you remember this movie. It looks familiar. How you don't remember our first movie we saw together. A lot of shit has happened during and after those years. What you trying to do is pick a fight with me because Brandon isn't here. "Seriously Tim". I'm very serious you cute when you mad tho, come here you need a hug. Stop playing with me Tim I'm a grown ass woman, but yes, I need a hug.

They both wrapped their arms around one another. Tim I really needed this. No problem ladybug I'm always here for you as he kisses her on the forehead. Look at me ladybug with his hand nudging under her chin, you have a little cheese on your lip, just when he was about to lean in for a passionate kiss the kids walked in with Brandon. Playing it off to a T; ladybug here the napkin get the cheese off your mouth. Thanks. Baby I thought you were with your brothers? I was but Elliott said neither of you was answering the phone, so I picked him up from his friend's house along with the other 3 kids. So, you telling me neither one of you heard your phone, that's kind of funny because I see you had the time to wear a bikini and eat nachos or maybe that's me thinking too far outside the box huh. Brandon, my phone is upstairs. I have been in the pool and in the living room all day. So how everything go with your brothers? Everything is great. I'm just wondering how your day went as he stared at her with a look of suspicion. My day went well. I can't complain. Yeah okay, Brandon responded. I'm going to the room to freshen up, Keisha said.

Tim can we talk for a second. Yeah, what's up? Have you noticed Keisha has been having a lot of mood swings? She definitely has been a little off lately. Do you think she's pregnant? How the fuck would I know you fucking her not me. Man, I know that. I'm only asking to see if this is how she was acting when she was pregnant with the kids. Yeah, but a lot of other shit came with it. Your girl still coming down? Yeah, I guess we had to push the date back; she couldn't get off of work. Okay cool when I get back next week hopefully by then we could meet her.

Let me talk to Keisha to figure out what's going on with her after that I'm meeting back up with my brothers if you want to hang out; yeah, I need to hang out. Keisha, Are you pregnant? Hell no, why would you ask me that of all things. Because you been acting differently lately so if you're not pregnant what the fuck is it. Nothing at all Brandon just trying to figure out some things. Figure out what things Keisha? Just some things. Things like what? Let me guess since you're on some bullshit: you don't want to marry me, you don't want another child, you still have feelings for your ex. Are you cheating on me Keisha? Get the fuck out my face Brandon for you to come up with that fuckery you just said is unbelievable. You know what I was trying to keep my thoughts to myself but since you want to push the envelope who the fuck are you talking? Who the fuck was you talking to the other day on the phone when you was in the bathroom talking about the shit getting hot?

Then you had the nerve to tell me you were talking about the damn water now who on some bullshit huh Brandon. Baby look I wasn't lying to you the water was too hot. I'll give you time to cool down, so Tim and I are going to chill with my brothers for a couples hours if you don't mind. Get the fuck out my face I'm not stupid you keep playing games just remember I can play games to.

What the fuck is that supposed to mean, Keisha? Exactly what I said now you read in between the lines. Yeah, alright you gonna get someone hurt I don't have time for this I'm out.

Chapter 35

"Brandon's Brothers"

Brandon yells "Tim I'm in the car "as he walks out the door. Tim gets in the car Brandon has the music blasting. Man turn that shit down what you tryna to do go deaf because I'm not. Do I need to drive? It doesn't seem like you're in the right state of mind just a quick observation. Man look she's tripping again you sure this not the same shit you went through when she was pregnant. Because I asked her if she was pregnant, she said no. Naw when Keisha and I were married she had ways to her but not like this. Maybe she is going through menopause. You funny as shit don't let her hear you say that. So, we're not dwelling on y'all

personal shit tonight are we because I
could have stayed in. No, I had to get
that off my chest before we met up
with my brothers.

Just to give you a heads up my
brothers they are some assholes
especially to people they just met. So,
don't let them know too much about
your personal business, keep that shit
short and sweet. Thanks, on the update
but you know I can handle my own.
Yeah, I know you handle your own, but
my brothers are a different kind of
breed, if they step out of line, I will
check them. Man look I'm out to enjoy
the night I don't have time for the
bullshit and as I say this in the most
respectful way there's no bitch in my
blood.

Brandon laughs with a smirk, things
that's understood don't need to be
explained. One of Brandon's brothers
called "B we here where are you?"
Man, Tim and I will be there in 10

minutes.

Who the fuck is Tim? Rodney chill the out Tim is family fall all the way the fuck back. "Who's family"? So, you go around claiming niggaz? You heard what I said fall back he's family tell my other brothers the same shit so there will not be a problem when we arrive, I will be there in a minute. They finally arrive at the bowling alley where Brandon's brothers reserved the bowling lane in the corner. What's up y'all ordered drinks and food already? Naw we didn't order food, but we had some drinks. Who the fuck is he? My name is Tim who the fuck are you fam? So, you Mr. Tough guy huh, Brandon I told you I don't like new people around me. Also, I told you to chill the fuck out on the phone did you forget fall back. To answer your indirect question, I'm definitely no tough guy, but I'm nobody bitch either. You got it Tim.

All this fucking tough guy shit let's see if you can bowl. So, let me ask you "Tim, how do you know my brother? Brandon is engaged to my ex-wife. So, you telling me Keisha is your ex, so how is that working out for you watching your ex fucking around with my brother. I'm not jealous at all. Yeah alright. Brandon you becoming soft how you hanging out with the ex-husband of your fiancée? Rodney asked. Where the fuck in this equation am I soft as Brandon approach Rodney? You became soft, you know how we do, nothing could get under your skin now look at you. Oh, really as Brandon punches Rodney in his mouth I told you stop playing with me. "Is this soft enough for you"? I told you don't disrespect me, or my relationship understand. Come on now Brandon, that's our brother, Tony said. Yeah, he's our brother but his bitch ass is out of line.

You know how he gets when he drinks. And that's why he got punched in his face. Fuck you Brandon while holding his mouth I would have fucked you up if I weren't drunk, Tony pass me another shot. Hell no! you done for tonight you tripping.

We didn't come down here for this bullshit Rodney we here to celebrate our brother's engagement. You right! I apologize bruh I was out of line I can own up to my faults. Tony, "Did you handle what I asked"? Brandon asked. Yeah, everything good. I can use some help booking everyone's flight back home for your wedding. Yeah, I know that's why I'm coming back home this Sunday to take some of the stress off your hands.

Tim I just beat your ass in bowling, yeah you won by 2 points Rodney well done. I'm ready to go, Brandon said. "Are you ready to go home already"? No! Let's go to a strip club or lounge.

Hell, yeah strip club it is. Tim since this is your neck of the woods you pick. Uh y'all act like I'm the strip club expert but I do have one in mind.

Oh, before we go are you sure Keisha is going to approve of you in a strip club. Yeah, Keisha's cool we have no secrets between us I will let her know when I go home. Yeah, Tim so what strip club are we going too? I forgot the name just follow us. They finally get to the strip club enjoying themselves throwing money like it's nothing. Rodney asks one of the strippers to give Brandon a lap dance.

While Brandon is drinking his whiskey, the stripper comes over so it's you getting married soon while she takes his cup out his hand and places it on the table. Baby girl I'm happily engaged soon to married and I will leave that way get your ass up off me. What you mean like this as she starts to twerk in front of him. I guess you don't

understand what I just said to you. Tim
switch seats with me. You will enjoy
the lap dance better than I would.
How you wanted to come here but not
enjoying the lap dance, Tony asked. I'm
enjoying myself but I can see the
scenery from afar. Keisha really
changed you huh bruh, Rodney said.
Yeah, she has changed me nothing or
no one is coming between that no other
woman is grinding on me but my wife.
So y'all can get any happy ending y'all
want while I finish my drink.
Aye Jamal walk with me to the bar.
"Did Tony tell you what we discuss"?
Yeah, he did. "Does Keisha know what's
going on"? Hell no! You know I can't
involve her in this, the less she knows
the better. You know how we get down
and what we into bruh she's a good
woman with kids you might need to
tell her. Yeah, I will in due time I'm just
not trying to lose my family.
I will do these last couple of hits and

I'm out of the game. You know it's not that easy bruh every time you say that you come right back to it you can't deny it's in your DNA. I gotta change for my family before shit hits the fan. That's why I moved away for a fresh start. Shit just getting too close to home.

You remember the FBI agent Jonathan that's been investigating us for years, especially me. Yeah why? He's dating Keisha's friend Tanya. "What the fuck how that happen"? She met him the same weekend I met Keisha, supposedly he was their limo driver when they came to the club. That shit is insane. I can't have this shit come back to Keisha or the kids, something happens to them, anything that walks in my path is dead. Brandon, we got this covered don't worry about it. Alright let's go see what these fools are doing.

Alright fellas what's the next move? Brandon asked. Man, I can eat shit we been drinking all night, Jamal responded. Shit down here close early then what we used to. So, I guess the only thing open is the breakfast restaurant right. Yeah, it's one around the corner about 5 minutes away. Shit I'm ordering everything on the menu, Jamal said while he laughed. After 2 hours of eating, talking and laughing everyone was tired and ready to go home. Remember tomorrow we have our suit fitting. Be on time and I made an appointment for this. What time tomorrow? At 12 noon.

You know damn well we been drinking all night 12 o'clock might be pushing it, Rodney said. I don't care drink water, but your ass betta be there by 12. Tim and Brandon finally make it home.

Chapter 36

"Not being Heard"

Next morning Keisha makes breakfast when Brandon comes downstairs "Good morning baby" yeah whatever "What you do last night"? and "What time did you come in"? We went bowling, to the strip club and grabbed something to eat. To be honest I didn't look at the time, but I guess around 3 or 4am. So, did you enjoy yourself last night because I damn sure didn't enjoy the way you left our conversation yesterday. Yeah, I had a good time. I hadn't seen my brothers in months what you mean the way I left the conversation. Why are you dismissing my feelings? What are you hiding from me? Keisha there's nothing I'm hiding from you why do you keep saying that. You know what I'm not about to sit and repeat myself you should already know. I'm not doing this with you today.

I have plans later this evening and need to be in a good head space to enjoy myself. So why do you need to be in a good headspace "Where are you going"? I'm going out. I guess I will tell you when I come in at 3 or 4 in the morning. So, who are you going out with? None of your business Brandon. You are my business what the fuck are you talking about, I'm not in the mood to play games with you who you are going out with.

Brandon the food on the stove if you're hungry as she sits at the table. Tim comes up from the basement. Man, I have a banging hangover. I need to take a shot and drink some water and eat something. Tim: So how did you like the strip club last night? Keisha asked.

Huh! As he whispered to Brandon in the kitchen you really told her you went to the strip club why in the hell would you do that. I told you I was going to tell her when we were at the bowling alley or were you that fucked up you don't remember. So, Tim you acting like you didn't hear my question. So, sense you both getting on my nerves this morning. I'm off duty. Let me elaborate on "off duty" mommy, fiancée, ex-wife, maid, problem solver, etc..... Do I need to say more? Also, tonight both of you are on children watch duties because I'm going out just to inform you Tim.

Damn Brandon what you do already it's only 10:30 in the morning. She's still pissed because she feels like I dismissed her feelings.

I was going to let her know the contractor called me to let me know I can move in this next weekend and my girl was able to move some things around to help.

Congratulations, I will pick a restaurant
for the double date to show my
appreciation and return the favor of
what you did for me and Ke. I gotta go.
I cannot be late as he calls his brothers.
Yo! Rodney you up? Kinda between
Tony and Jamal knocking on the door
and you calling. Be there on time, get
your ass up. Alright I'm up text me the
address.

Chapter 37

"The Reveal"

Brandon arrived at 11:30am still waiting for his brother's 5-10 minutes pass. Here they come at 11:58am walking in. What took y'all so long I said be on time. Chill bruh we still hung over and besides 11:58 is before 12 so we made it just in time, Jamal said. You have jokes, it's too early for it, Brandon responded. So, what is the color scheme? Store owner asked. I was thinking about maybe an ice grey suit for me and for my brothers ice blue suits. Okay will let me take everyone measurements also will you be purchasing shoes from us as well? It depends on what the shoes look like and how it complements our suits.

One more question: When is your wedding? July 20th. Oh! You only have six months left to get everything you need together. Well, you came to the right place. You should have everything back within 2-3 months since you ordered custom made suits.

Man, you have us looking like a fresh pack of winter fresh chewing gum, Rodney stated. Yeah, just make sure your ice cold and minty fresh when you walk down the aisle as Brandon brothers laughs. Today must be crack Brandon's balls; everyone looks good in their suits; you'll see how everything ties in the wedding. I hope Keisha and her bridesmaids have a better style and color because all of us are about to look minty fresh.

Do you know what Keisha bridesmaids look like? You can't have me walking down the aisle with some ugly duckling, you already setting me up with this damn color. I believe she has the two

young ladies I met in Vegas besides that
I don't know the other ladies. They're
cute but also off the market Tony and
Rodney.

Y'all always think someone wants y'all
always thinking with the wrong head
and wonder why you always in some
shit. My shit is under control don't
worry about what I do and who I do.
We need to sit down and talk. I already
informed Jamal about the FBI agent
who's been investigating us and how he
is now dating one of Keisha's friends.
Yeah, I remember him, but he has
nothing on us. So, what's the problem?
Did you not hear me say he's dating
one of Keisha's friends? This shit is
getting too close. After I do these hits
for Diablo, I'm out the game.

I'm no longer transporting weight,
making hits or anything else that
pertains to that lifestyle, I'm a family
man now. If Diablo has a problem with
it, I will personally deal with him

myself. You know Diablo is not that kind of guy that's just going to let you walk free, he's going to want something in return, Tony responded. Well, I have people watching him and his family routine. I play chess not checkers.

I have been Diablo hitman for 8 years. I know him inside and outside I will always beat him at his game, Brandon said. Yeah, but you know he doesn't play fair, family is not off limits with him, so he will try to hit you where it hurts, Rodney said. Brandon pulls out one of his burner phones. Look, I have a security camera installed in his home and in his cars with audio. However, and whenever you trying to execute this, we got your back.

B you need to tell Keisha. Not yet. Her and children's lives may be in danger if you miss hell all our lives will be in danger. When have you ever known me to miss? I will tell her soon I need to find the right time. There will never be

a right time to tell her you're a hitman
that transports weight and the shot
caller for our organization. You right I
will tell her after we get married.
Either way I may lose my family now
that I think about.

Shit I have been holding this secret for
about 2 years and she already expresses
to me she doesn't like secrets or being
lied to and that's just what I did. In a
way I'm putting her right back through
the same shit Tim did just not on the
cheating shit but worst.

Did it ever cross your mind to tell her
before it got this far? Jamal asked.
Several times laying in bed next to her
I wanted to, but I held back. But she
knew something was wrong. How the
hell do I bounce back from this? I'm in
way too deep. Out of all the women
you brought home, Keisha is the only
one mom likes and that's saying a lot.
Yeah, that's why I'm not trying to lose
her. Well at some point bruh she will

figure this out there's nothing stupid about her.

To be honest with you, maybe you need to tell her before you walk down the aisle because once you say "I DO" there's no turning back. Now all her assets will be tied into your illegal activities especially when you have federal agents breathing down our necks. True but I was looking at it like this: Under the spouse privilege that is recognized by the court. If it ever gets to a point, she needs to testify against me, she couldn't because we're married. So, you just have this all planned out? Rodney said. At this moment yeah but anything could change. I will catch up with y'all later. What will we do with our brother? It seems like his vision is blurred. He really needs to think about the consequences that we all are about to endured with his impulsive decision. Rodney and Tony, did you know he was watching Diablo house? Jamal asked.

Yeah, he mentioned it last time he was home, but I brushed it off how many times Brandon told you he wanted out and he didn't do it, Rodney said. The fire in his eyes today for once I actually believe him. When we fly back home, we gotta discuss this with our other brothers especially while Brandon is there. Sounds like a plan. I need some sleep. This hangover is nothing to play with.

Chapter 38

"Ladies Night Out"

Several hours later Keisha finally gets dressed to have a fun girls night out while Brandon is staring at her. So, did you figure out where you and the ladies are going? Maybe a strip club. Who knows where we're gonna to end up? I guess where our cars take us as she laughs. Aye Ke yes baby umm I just wanted to say you look very pretty. Thanks. Keisha meets up with the ladies at a lounge dancing the night away until she sits down having a drink or two.

Tanya comes over can we talk about the last time "I deeply want to apologize for our fall out. I accept your apology and I'm sorry too. Never did I want us to be in this kind of space, love you girl, Keisha said. Tonight, is all about us and having a fun weekend, girl my house is driving me insane. Tim finally went to court and had a paternity test done in which he is the father of Timothy. I believe Brandon is keeping some secrets and of course the children just all over the house cannot wait for them to go back to school.

I'm sorry Tanya, I just needed to vent. No problem! Tanya pulled Keisha's hand and headed to the dance floor. This sexy young guy came behind Keisha to dance. Little did she know Brandon's brothers were at the same lounge watching.

They all walked up to them. You probably want to take your hands off my brother's wife asap. Man, you bugging we just dancing, yeah that's the problem step the hell off.

This is fucking ridiculous. "Did Brandon send you guys here to spy on me"? No!

Brandon doesn't even know we here this is our last night before we leave tomorrow. How is everything going with my nieces and nephews? They are driving me up a wall. I'm counting down the days when school starts. Shid I understand that. How is my baby brother treating you? I love your brother so much but lately he's just been so secretive, and I just can't put my finger on it.

I would catch him looking at me and when I asked him what's wrong, he would say nothing wrong. Not to make excuses for him but he has moments when he's trying to figure out things. One thing about my brother he's deeply in love with you to the point he would drink your bath water, Tony said.

So, I guess the next time I will see you sis is at the wedding huh? Yeah. So, who is this young lady Keisha? Oh, I'm sorry Tanya is my business partner, best friend, bridesmaid. Let me introduce you to Tanya. This is Jamal, Tony, and Rodney, Brandon's brothers. Nice to meet you.

So, I'm walking down the aisle with her right, Rodney said with a smile. I haven't made matches with who's walking down with who yet. Okay I just put my bid in. Whatever Rodney. It's time to bounce; we have four hours before we need to be at the airport. Keisha, will you be okay? If not, we can follow you home. No, I'm fine but thanks. Yeah, it's getting late "Tanya you ready"? Yeah, tomorrow is going to be a long workday.

Chapter 39

"The Confession"

She finally makes it home. She jumps in the shower Brandon walks in the bathroom.

Baby, did you have a great time? Yes, I did. I really need to talk to you about something serious. Can it wait until I get out of the shower or tomorrow? Yeah, I will tell you when I come back from Vegas. Baby I'm sorry I'm just so tired. He's holding her while laying in the bed and whispering to her I love you. He really couldn't wait until he came back from Vegas like he agreed to. Baby there's something you need to know about me.

She dozed in and out of sleep baby did you say something. Yeah, I need to tell you something profoundly serious about me. I don't want you to judge me and I don't want to lose you or the children but I'm a…………. Just when he was about to say it, she started to snore. He kisses her on the forehead and whispers hopefully, you still love me.

He leaves a note on the nightstand:

To My heartbeat,

When I first met you, I knew there was something different that I couldn't shake about you. From the time that we said we were officially together every decision that I made was for us whether right or wrong. You are my soulmate, my peace, my backbone, my everything, words cannot explain. Everything you know about me is true and honest feelings towards you and the kids down to some parts of my business. After I confess to you what I have been holding for almost 2 years. Please forgive me. I tried to tell you last night, but you fell asleep. This is something I prefer to tell you in person, not over the phone or in this letter. See you in a couple of days MY LOVE.

Love, Brandon